The Sol Plaatje European Union
Poetry Anthology

Volume IV

Selected by Ingrid de Kok, Johann de Lange
and Goodenough Mashego

The views and opinions expressed in this publication are not necessarily those of the funder.

First published by Jacana Media (Pty) Ltd in 2014

10 Orange Street
Sunnyside
Auckland Park 2092
South Africa
+2711 628 3200
www.jacana.co.za

© Individual authors, 2014

All rights reserved.

ISBN 978-1-4314-2025-4

Cover design by Shawn Paikin
Cover image © Dylan Culhane
Set in Ehrhardt 11/13pt
Printed and bound by Creda Communications
Job no. 002363

See a complete list of Jacana titles at www.jacana.co.za

The Sol Plaatje European Union
Poetry Anthology

Volume IV

Contents

Foreword *Dr Mongane Wally Serote* ix
Message from the ambassador *Roeland van de Geer* . . . xiii

Born and Died, Lived *Jim Pascual Agustin* 1
Illegal, Undocumented *Jim Pascual Agustin* 3
Dust *Kyle Steven Allan* 5
The Sun's Heart *Kyle Steven Allan* 7
The Grail *Adewole Armah* 9
By Heart *Saaleha Idrees Bamjee* 11
Kisses *Saaleha Idrees Bamjee* 12
Secret *Saaleha Idrees Bamjee* 14
email to the ancestors *Suzan-Jane Kathleen Bell* 15
Mfowethu, The rockdriller is not dead
Suzan-Jane Kathleen Bell 16
Horn Screaming *Ayanda Billie* 19
the clown lady *Fadwah Booley* 20
Mother's Lyric (i) *Sindiswa Busuka* 22
Sobriety and Grief *Sindiswa Busuka* 24
Letters from shallow graves *Zethu Cakata* 26
Life lessons *Ntyatyi Christian* 27
The Companion *Margaret Clough* 28
Flames *Margaret Clough* 29
Palm Sunday *Margaret Clough* 31
Dreaming of Soccer *Christine Coates* 32
The story of how I love a river *Christine Coates* 35

The Heart of the Matter *Lise Day* 36
Rhinos *Gail Dendy* 37
Suitcase *Gail Dendy* 38
Whisker *Gail Dendy* 39
The survival kit *Abigail George*. 41
Koorsboom *Sunelle Geyer* 42
Fever tree *Sunelle Geyer* 43
Ma says *Chantelle Gray* 44
All the Men *Kerry Hammerton* 45
The Moment *Kerry Hammerton* 47
water rising *Kerry Hammerton* 48
Politics in Parliament *Vernon R.L. Head* 50
The limited attractions of Australia for the
elderly and the dead *Colleen Higgs* 51
Animals are the evidence *Sandra Hill* 52
Love in the time of extinction *Sandra Hill*. 54
Beautiful *Rochelle Jacobs* 55
Dear Dad *Rochelle Jacobs* 56
Something Other *Rochelle Jacobs* 58
Children Watching Old People *Thabo Jijana* 60
Grandma's People *Thabo Jijana* 61
The Thing about Mugabe *Thabo Jijana*. 62
How does a marriage die? *Justine Joseph*. 64
Soap *Justine Joseph* 68
Kokwana u fambile – Grandmother is gone
Moses Nzama Khaizen. 70
The Spring Rains *Moses Nzama Khaizen* 71

13 December 2013 *Gertrude Trudi Makhaya*	74
Misfathered *Gertrude Trudi Makhaya*	78
Semputšiše *Katise Mawela*	80
Don't Ask Me *Katise Mawela*	81
rough draft *Frank Meintjies*	82
Letter from Marikana *Komiso Mfingo*	83
Letter from Marikana *Komiso Mfingo*	85
i know a guy *Andrew Miller*	87
Devil's Fish *Janine Jocelyn Milne*	88
Eulogy *Janine Jocelyn Milne*	90
Train *Janine Jocelyn Milne*	92
Kankere, o selo mang? *Jackie Mondi*	93
Cancer, what the hell are you? *Jackie Mondi*	95
Scenes from India I – Beautiful *Nedine Moonsamy*	97
Scenes from India II – A Walk into the Park *Nedine Moonsamy*	99
Circumference, Lion's Head *Nick Mulgrew*	101
a June missive *Nick Mulgrew*	103
'n meisie wat in haar kamer dans *Eduan Naudé*	105
a girl dancing in her room *Eduan Naude*	106
Bushbaby *Pam Newham*	107
Mother in a glass with ice *Pam Newham*	108
Pistachios *Pam Newham*	109
Please stop the music *Sizakele Nkosi*	111
Xenophobic Society *Lazola Pambo*	113
The Heartbeat *Thabo Seseane*	114
#6 *Francine Simon*	115

#8 *Francine Simon* 116
After she is taken home, I watch the news
Annette Snyckers 117
Away *Annette Snyckers* 118
China *Dianne Stewart* 119
The Dancer in Flamenco Strikes *Jan Tromp* 120
Zebra Express *Jan Tromp* 123
adamastor wakes *Susan Woodward* 125
lights out *Susan Woodward* 126
The Captured Maiden *Sithembele Xhengwana* 128
Hintsa's Portrait *Sithembele Xhengwana* 131

Biographies 133
About the European Union 149

Foreword

South Africa is an old poetic country. In her being a poetic country, she is as old as life, language and fire. Life is 4 billion years, and its beginning in Barberton, a small town in Mpumalanga – the place of the rising sun – is just a miracle, found as a singular cell in a rock. But life cannot do, it can burst like a bubble, if it is without language – another miracle – how does language form, articulate, express consciousness and eventually lead to all kinds of actions: some actions which sustain life, some which destroy it. It is strange, it is incomprehensible at times, and more of a mind-boggling truth that actually, if there was no heat, no warmth, no fire, life would just shrivel like a cover of a seed, turn to dust, just be there to incubate other seeds, and their coverings. Everything – life, language and fire – are so fragile yet so present! Fire starts with two sticks and grass and bursts to life and death. It was first started in life, science tells us in Wonderwerk cave in Northern Cape near Kuruman, where the great quiet Sanusi, Credo Mutwa and Virginia now live.

This country, our country is just a poet, the original poet, she speaks and sings and dances, as if forever and she asks, do the poets hear, see, feel, taste and do they touch me? The poets do – relentlessly in this *Sol Plaatje European Union Poetry Anthology*: They rivet their spiritual eye on her, trying to hold her rivers, oceans, breeze, sunlight, trees, grass, soil, landscapes and everything – they hold on to them firmly so that they can, with all their senses understand the country, its people, landscapes and things which it is. But there are also those things which one cannot see with the eye. There is pain galore of mothers especially and fathers whose pain is misunderstood; there is the pain of children who do not understand why it is that they were brought here to earth, to do what?

The scanning inner eye of the poets miss nothing – fowls, zebras, elders are caught in this bird's-eye-view camera, which freezes them forever for the coming generations which may not know, but will have to know because, even as the information technology is now referred to in the poems, the best of the record, about the best and the worst, is still the domain of human creation, experience and interpretation – the spirit of the creation of the creator.

How does a marriage die?
mine died slowly
first the teeth fall out
– Justine Joseph (How does a marriage die?)

A good example of someone
who sleeps very well
After doing inappropriate things
all day every day
Is grandma's rooster
Casually climbing down
off a fowl: as if releasing himself
from a handshake
gone longer
than necessary …
– Thabo Jijane (Grandma's People)

> *What can he mean? And who is he?*
> *What does he want? Why does he care?*
> *He never speaks; he only follows me*
> *and when I turn there's nothing I can see.*
> – Margaret Clough (The Companion)

She knows something about who he is … "always following …" her they know each other, they know about the breeze, the grass, the sea, as do ghosts or spirits.

> *No one listens, you might as well follow Ingrid into the*
> *ocean at Three Anchor Bay, whispers one voice.*
> *The voice subsides –*
> *The white tablet courses through your veins*
> – Fadwah Booley (The Clown Lady)

Something has snapped, something has gone wrong in with 'The Clown Lady'; Ingrid Jonker one of the greatest South African poets, when that happened, she walked into the sea and vanished. Maybe there were no white tablets then, or, if there were, Ingrid felt she did not need them.

The myriad tapestries in this collection of poems, by South African and other Southern African poets, is splashed into our minds and spirits. Reading them is a great revelation of the South African diversity of landscape, people, beliefs, religions, culture and as always the poets have never found these to be threatening – at worst the poets wonder at this diversity at best, they allow the diversity to reveal its voices to us and we hear it speak in tongues.

We must also remember as we read these poems, which are in harmony with the diverseness of the landscape of this most beautiful country, that at times, most times, these poems are also performed.

The new generation of South African poets write in one language, translate the poem into another language, write and perform, at times sing the poems.

The poets have also captured the unease, the restlessness, the disquiet, the search which the land, which in times of climate change, seems to allow the seasons to go around change temperaments, attitudes and what they are expected to do.

Read 'The Clown Lady' by Fadwah Booley and be told about how the distance we have travelled now articulates itself to us. Hear Ayanda Billie's 'Horn screaming' and then also, the poets write emails to the ancestors.

Ask Suzan-Jane Kathleen Bell how that is done. If we go by Billie and Bell, they know that South Africa with its myriad religious denominations, is also a spiritual country, so also says Bamjee, ask Mawela too!

The poems in this collection are full of life. They do not let life goof it, they hold onto it knowing that all the miracles of being are in it, and the lessons to know oneself are in it, it is, this life, life and living.

The best place of education to educate consciousness, which educate expression, which educate actions – read 'Zebra Express', when life in beauty also expresses the dangers of life.

Dr Mongane Wally Serote

Message from the ambassador

In a world deeply affected by the impacts of the 2008 global financial crisis, culture has in many cases been one of the first casualties of austerity measures and budget cuts.

I would argue, however, that the financial crisis has shown us that development based solely on economic and financial imperatives is an illusion. Neither financial capital nor natural resources alone shape the future of societies and states. Human capital is key and if we are to emerge stronger from this crisis, we must not forget the human element – and culture is of course central to this.

I am proud that the European Union Delegation to South Africa, in line with the *Conclusions of the Council of the European Union in November 2008 on the promotion of cultural diversity and intercultural dialogue in the external relations of the Union and its Member States*, has managed over the past few years to maintain its support for culture.

The Delegation, together with the EU Member States represented in South Africa and the European Union National Institutes for Culture (EUNIC), continues to support a range of cultural initiatives and actions, one of these being the *Sol Plaatje European Union Poetry Competition and Anthology*. For the fourth year running it has been particularly gratifying to support this wonderful initiative which celebrates South Africa's multilingual society by inviting poets to submit their contributions in any of the country's official languages. This surely makes the initiative quite unique.

In 2014, and as previously in partnership with the Jacana Media Foundation, a superb poetry anthology has again seen the light of day. I can only hope that South Africans from all walks of life will continue to show their support by acquiring this varied collection of South African works. May it continue to contribute to South Africa's efforts to promote a greater appreciation and love of its many languages and cultures.

Roeland van de Geer
EU Ambassador to South Africa

Born and Died, Lived

1904 is all I know. Not the day
or month she was born. Not even
her real name. She was "Lola"
to everyone. I could never imagine her
as my father's mother. Or a woman

who got up to get dressed after sex.
Her underwear was the size
of a butterfly net, flag of surrender
on a wire wash line. She was
quiet most of the time,

her teeth red with betel nut. Soft
munching while she watched
over us who feigned snores at *siesta*.
Her blouse was shorter
than her *kamison*, with sleeves

like lace wings. I liked pressing
my fingers between the embroidery,
pink dots of skin against white.
She wore skirts the colour of mud,
if not outright black, so long

the ends dragged pebbles.
They kept her feet untouched
by sunlight. Once I saw her
bathe by the river. Wrinkled
back as if studded with diamonds.

Then she let her hair fall
all the way past the line left by her
underwear garter. Smooth
and round, the stones under
her feet shimmered.

JIM PASCUAL AGUSTIN

Illegal, Undocumented

The light from your helmet
flickers to fading. The eyes

of the other miners, stars
as the sky clouds over.

You have lost count of the days
underground. You can no longer tell

who is trying to stifle a cough.
Dwarfed by the growing darkness,

memory takes your earth-encrusted hand
to a place where ferns dampen

your skin as you run, the shrill
cries of birds and vervets

filling the air. But you know
only the rough faces

of rocks surround you,
silent and still as minerals

that have lost all value.
You dare not move

a breath as voices
depart. The ladder

to the surface they leave,
a new trap.

JIM PASCUAL AGUSTIN

Dust

"Schoolkids beat thug to death!"

"Find your true love!"

"Man discovers he has been married for ten years!
Without his knowledge!"

Third paper shows our president unveiling
A lifesize statue of Albert Luthuli,

Former president of the ANC and Nobel
prize winner.
Below the caption is quoted

"We are all children of Luthuli"

Luthuli makes me think of the isiZulu word for dust,
uthuli. I see in my mind
A world full of dry dust. Farmers

Turning up dust in their dry hands. My warm
Hands full of dust. Sun is shining

Outside, traffic flowing in the city
Of choice. Luthuli is warm, human, clanned,

But its basic substance, the root, is uthuli,
The dust of our being. A torment and a need.

A gift and a silence. Luthuli's name is as real as
this land,
And open in meaning.

Hot outside. Dust outside. People walking past,
Looking into the shop as they go past.

I turn back to the first paper.
It shows the brown naked body of the thug lying in
the dust,

With the high school students who beat him to death
Looking on
Triumphant headline saying

"Pupil justice! Schoolkids beat thug to death!"
On the front page of the newspaper.

The day passes before my eyes in a haze of images
after this.
Images that you won't find in newspapers.

KYLE STEVEN ALLAN

The Sun's Heart

The sun's heart is found inside
the earth. You will smell
the sun when you dig soil
up to plant seeds, take
out weeds or bury someone.
You will smell the sun
on a hot day when
the heat penetrates
every building,
entering your bones
and making you cry out
with exhaustion,
the heat
rising up through
miles of buried soil,
compressed remains of
forgotten and dead cities,
the dark foundations of skyscrapers
reaching to the clouds
and saying nothing
as their glass reflects
a simulacrum of
eternity.
You will smell the sun
on the backs of tyres
made of synthetic rubber
at 10 o'clock
outside Sifafa action bar,
mixed with dirt
and oil.

You smell it even in an
apartment in the middle
of a conversation about
war, radio controlled
drones, and everyone is drunk,
and the dj interrupts his
Saturday night radio mix
to flight an advert
about instant messaging,
called by some bbm, or
whatsapp.

    KYLE STEVEN ALLAN

The Grail

From the Grail of overflowing grief
I should take my cue:
The faces of mourners and pallbearers
Are the Eden where ripe elegies have fallen. . .

Father, I don't speak with the tongue
Of humanity. I surf through cadences
Of ghosts and knock at doors of the underworld
Where I ask for the chalice of my broken boyhood.
And I still want to drink my youth to dregs.

I'm Telemachus streaking across the skies
Of your absence; the once chubby boy
Who feared you. I feared you, father,
So much so when 'I was fat like a woman'.
Your hoarse voice and high-pitched laugh
Still echo off the walls of my heart. And
It's not the report of the gun that moved
Me to tears, but your grey face when
Your last bead of sweat touched earth.

You forgot to ride your favourite horse
To your forebears; you called him *Sula*,
Sul' iinyembezi zabathakathi: wipe the tears
Of wizards, of those who shout incantations
Into spiders' webs, who tell these web-spinners
To nibble at us when we've fallen into torpor.

The village people said: 'The man is dead.
His 9mm parabellum brought his demise.
He lay on his bed, and looked in the mirror
Before he shouted an order to his gun.
This truth shall the loving son and brother
Tell his next of kin.'

That day still bangs about in the corridors of my ears;
And I've drunk from many cups of tears in this life,
Yet I know the Grail won't contain my tears forever.

ADEWOLE ARMAH

By Heart

As a child, I learnt things
off by heart.
Private angels worked
under the skin of my chest
scratching prompts on pulsing tissue.
In the afternoons at madrasa
I prayed with sounds
from engraved organs repeating
after the moulana Arabic letters
starting their lives in different
parts of my throat. *Don't mix them up*
he said *You could be saying Dog
instead of Heart.*
The meanings of other things
he did not teach, crafting for us
sacred chants only
God would understand.
As an adult, I had to look
again to my heart
the places in my throat
the angels left
their tools scattered blindly
I bent to pick one up.

        SAALEHA IDREES BAMJEE

Kisses

On this hill in another country
my eyes closed to the sun on my face
the grass is a lovers' first touch
soft against the back of my neck
and I think of all the boys I kissed.

I remember the first time.
The awkward insistence
the disappointment no one writes about
squashed against a cold car
next to the track field at Wits
while everyone else crammed for exams.
Let me tell you something, don't kiss anyone
because you want to get it over with.
That type of kiss you never get over.

The second one was more considerate.
He'd had too much practice, that was telling.
It cost R20 to buy the silence of the maid
hovering close to the couch, cleaning while we clinched.

The third kiss I gave was cruel.
It was only to prove I felt nothing for him
at his cousin's wedding in the pitch of the car park
where no one could see. In that dark, I was ugly.

And then there was the one
who kissed me to tell me it was over.
His tongue sliced me into ribbons
and left me clotting in the seat
of an empty movie theatre.

Now on this hill in another country
my mouth full of cheese and grapes
I think of the man I've yet to kiss
for whom I'll take back
gifts of perfume and chocolate.

SAALEHA IDREES BAMJEE

Secret

We were eight.
You made me hold your secret.
Squeezed my fingers around it.
Fused the joints, knitted the skin.
It's now twelve years.
They tell me you're a good mother.
I'll know it when I see your children
with each of their palms open to the world.
This useless fist, it should have broken
years ago, smashed through shame
and the man in the sweet shop.
Look, I'm still holding your secret.

                SAALEHA IDREES BAMJEE

A sonnet remix titled:
email to the ancestors

June wind songs weep for //Kabbo's lost feet

the moon rolls, finds Bitterpits, out roll the dead

growling skies greet forgotten lives that meet

baboons from clouds drop as insect jazz beats shed

clouds burst wearing long legs bringing good rain

water bulls and ostrich shells dance alone

Karoo silence changed, bright light the same

fingers run across an eland in stone

a white boulder at //Kabbo's touch sighs

finder of his father's father's sacred spring

a lone jackal buzzard high above flies

land renamed Arbeidsvreug, a strange new thing

//Kabbo sprints to Brinkkop chasing the curved horns of the moon

and springbok leaps to his returning tune

SUZAN-JANE KATHLEEN BELL

Mfowethu, *The rockdriller is not dead*
[Rooikoppies 16 August 2012]

Mfowethu,
The rockdriller is not dead

The hills are red this autumn
cowards shot them in the back

47 brave hearts carved from platinum at rooikoppies,
between Rustenberg and Brits

Mfowethu,
The rockdriller is not dead

They are ezinyoni / birds in a tree
Where Thembinkosi Gwelani asks:
"What do I see?"

And Dumisani Mthinti answers:
"It is a man with a gun."

"We see umshini wam held up high by the policemen in blue," they chorus

Paulina Masuhlo sings:
"Let us run."
Daluvuyo Bongo sings:
"Let us hide."

Mafolisi Mabiya sings:
"We are not afraid of them."
Thobisile Zimbambele and Thabiso Mosebetsane sing:
"We are not afraid of them."

All 34 birds and more sing: "We are not afraid of them."

Exploding, exploding, the gun powder explodes / Qhu,
Qhu saqhuma isibhamu
precious lives for precious metals
"I am finished" cries the madala rockdriller, boots
bloodied red,
cowering behind a rock

34 silent birds fall from the tree

Mfowethu,
The rockdriller is not dead

Marakane miners, like Maqoma's ghost,
Will rise from the dust of Rooikoppies
between Rustenburg and Brits

No more tinker, tailor, policeman, saviour
Rich man, poor man, rockdriller, thief
Big house, little house, jondolo, slaps

The blood of a rockdriller, no different to a manager,
 rocks our land

Mfowethu,
The rockdrillers are not dead

Their message lives on

> *Rooikoppies means 'red hills' in Afrikaans. Rooikoppies, also known as Marikana, is a town in the Rustenburg local municipality, Bojanala Platinum District Municipality in the North West province of South Africa.*

SUZAN-JANE KATHLEEN BELL

Horn Screaming
to Zim Ngqawana

I feel your horn screaming
Vadzimu
        Vadzimu
Where noise is silenced
Screams trapped
With a note,

I feel it in the air
Ingoma yakho
Combining restless souls
In *Zimphonic Suites*
"Mayenzeke intando yakho,"

Zimology
Your spirit crowds me
In your *San songs*
Defying the madness
Smashing our inner-man,

Zim-Zim
This way we live
With you
The star that shines
Qula Afrika.

        AYANDA BILLIE

the clown lady

Golden Arrow bus terminus, Terminal D2, Ocean View/
Retreat, Grand Parade, Cape Town
Wednesday, 31 July 2013

When you look in the mirror,
there is your face –
shining back,
much older, unrecognisable.
Nothing tethers you to the once youthful, wondrous girl you
were.
The years slipped by in secret
but time's mark etched in each deep line and wrinkle strewn
across your face.
Your calloused, leathery hand reaches for a brush.
You close your eyes and
Van Gogh begins to paint –
blue, pink, purple, red,
blue, pink, purple, red,
blue, pink, purple, red;
scarlet lips for a lady,
maybe a smile to mask the pain.
Before you leave the house you remember to take your
medication –
a pink tablet to stave off the madness,
a white tablet to *drain away the voices,*
a yellow tablet for the blues.
You catch a taxi to Cape Town,
Sisiphus drags your bag of skeletons down the steps from
the taxi rank to the Grand Parade –
He's used to pushing rocks up the hill (you think).

You sit at bus terminal D2, Ocean View/ Retreat –
light a cigarette,
pick at peanut skins,
howl profanities at passing bus patrons,
the newspaper lady shouting "Son mummy Son", "Voice mummy Voice",
bergies,
Somalian street vendors,
your Khoisan ancestors,
the spirits of Jan van Riebeeck and company.
A little girl stares at you quizzically, tugs on her mother's dress, points to you and says "mummy look at the clown lady."
No one listens, you might as well follow Ingrid into the ocean at Three Anchor Bay, whispers one voice.
The voice subsides –
the white tablet courses through your veins.

FADWAH BOOLEY

Mother's Lyric (i)

Under two things the earth trembles, under three it cannot bear up:

the barren womb.

This is Formation

This is a gardener   this is a man of faith   this is feverish ground

Two small burning hands

    held close to her breast

    head on her knees   burrowed beneath the earth

    my young bulb   asleep beneath the roots of bluebells

This is fevered ground

this is how the earth swells

this is the soils' hot breath meeting the chill

See the small gelatine skull   feel the soft ridges of the spine

    hear the bloom of each pore

This is the form I once knew

this was the form

Where were you   when I turned her eyeless face east

                said the man of faith

Where were you   when I rooted lilies for eyes   said the gardener

This is the bruised tongue   this is the boneless answer
this is the tightly coiled
      whisper.

                        SINDISWA BUSUKA

Sobriety and Grief

He lives in a house with a red Rolls Royce
and says the doctor's trying to kill him.
He's seventy-eight. I'm thirteen. And I can't seem to
sober up for his death.

He's been dying for two years now, you see
"So what did you eventually do?" Fran asked.
"Nothing," I told her.
"I waited for it stoned."

While dying he wanted me home in the early hours.
"Why? I mean, what happened?"
"He died. And mom cried.
And I stood in the doorway. Waiting."

"For what?"
"Sobriety and grief," I replied.

Neither decided to arrive as I walked over to him.
"Have you ever spoken about this to anyone?
You never speak about this stuff,
not even to me."

"What for?"
"I don't know? Closure or something?"

Well, a fancy woman from a fancy funeral parlour
tried to share the Five Stages of Grief with us.
Called herself a grief counsellor
then she called him 'the deceased'.

And there she was counselling us from a clipboard.
Burial or cremation? Memorial or wake?
Coffin – chestnut, oak or pine?
Cash or card? We don't do cheques.

And all I could say is his name is not 'deceased'.
"She replied, 'This is very good.
I see you've arrived
at stage 1:
Denial.'"

                              SINDISWA BUSUKA

Letters from shallow graves

My dear comrade
It's me whose grave was shallowly dug
One Thursday evening
When my brutal end came
And prematurely my farewell was held
Nice and short as everyone was on the run
I write to you from the bush still
In Botswana
In Maseru
In Harare
In Lusaka
I am happy you made a safe return
Remember to ensure that
No child will ever have his bones
Lie where mine are lying
Yearning for fruits of a free land

                          ZETHU CAKATA

Life lessons

we chant the different colours of rain
recite the names of our forgotten foremothers
account for their missing cattle
make peace with this land

we learn to embrace the ailing body
forgive it

dislodge the scars!

we unlearn our skins
relearn ourselves

we learn to forgive the fathers
love ourselves
and forgive ourselves for their not loving us

we bless the ever yielding sky for giving rain

Oh! Child of dreamers
Bless this earth

How we love to live!

                    NTYATYI CHRISTIAN

The Companion

There is someone always following me.
I'm sure, I'm sure, there's someone there.
but when I turn, there's nothing I can see.

In the soft rustle of the dry leaves of a tree
and in the sighing grasses I can hear
there's someone always following me.

Sometimes when walking by the sea,
the splashing of his feet tells me he is near,
but when I turn there's nothing I can see.

However fast I run I cannot flee.
I try to hide away, but everywhere
I go there's someone following me.

That sound like the faint buzzing of a bee –
he's breathing at my back. I fear
to turn, although there's nothing I can see.

What can he mean? And who is he?
What does he want? Why does he care?
He never speaks; he only follows me
and when I turn there's nothing I can see.

MARGARET CLOUGH

Flames

Making the fire was my job,
Dad supervising from his easy chair.
"The logs must criss-cross to allow
for air beneath. Don't roll
the newspaper. It must be crunched.
The kindling sticks are far too green.
Go out into the yard and
get some more."

I was an expert while
still small enough to scramble in
the crawl-space where the wood was kept.

I would kneel down on the hearthrug,
to coax a tiny flicker, until
encouraged by my blowing,
it sprang up, grew into a wild yellow beast,
that licked the piled up wood,
began to roar, and claw
its way towards the chimney.

Then I would sit back and bask,
while warmth spilled from the grate, until
it filled the room and breath
no longer fogged the windowpanes.

But now it seems
I am incompetent.
Can't even be allowed
to light a candle.
I have become
too doddery for naked flames,
too old to play with fire.

MARGARET CLOUGH

Palm Sunday

A strong surge of foreign voices bursts
from the small stone building and brings
a cool blessing to the busy streets.
White gulls swoop above us. A breeze
carries the scent of seaweed
and the corner café's baking.
A Malawian choir leads our small procession
swaying with songs that speak of home

At the beginning of this sad and sacred week
we learn to hold less tightly to
the small crosses that we bear.

      MARGARET CLOUGH

Dreaming of Soccer

I grew up on the edge of District Six, all we had was a ball;
newspapers taped round and round.
The Malay boys had a leather ball; their dad's drapers and tailors,
and matches in the street, teaming ourselves, until the muezzin called
them to prayers and our mothers yelling to come for supper.
Dreaming of soccer, how I dribbled the ball,
how I passed it to Desmond Green and he back to me,
how I shot it into the back of the net.
Darling Street, late afternoon, the hill, a short cut.
Bergies slept there under the milkwoods, they ate boys,
like the Sabbath chicken, spitting out the bones, Mom said.
Hansel bones.
The sun low between Lion's Head and Devil's Peak,
a blink of an eye, a bogey winking, a candle.
Then I saw the glass, the rounded ends of bottles.
But I was nimble, I was quick like Desmond Green,
Hubbly Bubbly, Pepsi, Coca-Cola,
a window for empties at the bottle store,
a tickey a bottle, a sixpence for whiskey,
a miracle I told Desmond,
from under the milkwoods, money for our own ball.
The Malay boys, as good as them, a proper team,
like the story in shul, manna in the desert, pansella.

Shifren's Sports Shop smells of leather and rubber,
delivery bikes with fat black tyres, Raleigh racers,
rows of balls, oval rugby balls,
netballs, tennis balls, ping-pong balls and a brown leather ball,
a round leather ball.
Mr Shifren counted the coins, 'I'm not Father Christmas you know',
but he took it from the high shelf.
The Malays goaded, 'Trying for Moroka Swallows?'
We settled on Sundays – they couldn't play Fridays,
our Saturdays Sabbath.

Years later, tough years, lean years, the stock market-crashed years.
I walked the cities begging for work,
it was a Friday, the start of sunset,
and I was to bring a shabbas chicken for the table, but my hands were empty.
At Rietvlei I parked the car near milkwoods and ran the motor, the gas fumes –
perhaps if I died.
The shades under the afternoon trees lengthened,
then – a glint, a wink of an eye. Their magnified lenses.
The days of street soccer rollicking back to save me.
I drove to Bothasig Main Street, to Solly's on the corner,
and I could buy a chicken, a large roaster,
and a bar of chocolate.

In the street I met Desmond – it had been thirty years.
He came home for supper, for chicken and challah,
and, as I was carving the meat, and he was drinking whiskey
he offered me a new job.

                              CHRISTINE COATES

The story of how I love a river[*]

This is the story of how I love a river –
how I float on gold-brown water
to the open mouth of the sea rippling brown,
water from far flowing
glows like glass,
sand sifted gold,
how I plunge my body,
allow it to turn and be carried headlong
or spin around,
watch my feet lead me to the sea,
how cold blue water meets warm brown,
waves running, and the incoming tide
swirl and eddy.
How the rocks, sand dug away,
create rapids.
how I lie long and flat – how terns on the bank lift
and, how, like all my worries,
they are bits of torn paper
swirling up and away.

CHRISTINE COATES

---

[*] The title is a nod to Ted Hugh's poem *Arethusa*; 'Tales from Ovid',
 Faber and Faber 1997.

The Heart of the Matter

Today I cooked an artichoke
which is really a bitter thing
needing garlic for sweetness,
oil for softness, lemon for zing.

I eat it in the evening hush
after a day of swirling wind
from each petal
scrape the good
discard the tip of gall.
I think it's like my life –
outer leaves leathery
resilient as my youth,
the inner segments
mushy middle-age.
Then, suddenly the choke,
a hairy knob of awfulness
I incise it carefully
discard it chop chop.

Now relish the succulent
sweet heart of maturity,

and the best part
of an artichoke is,
all that comes after
tastes even better.

LISE DAY

Rhinos

We carry aphrodisiacs on our snouts –
or so they say. A rumpled carpet is,
in fact, our skin. We have pinhole eyes,

relatively speaking, and rumps the size
of freezer chests. We could pack entire houses
with our volume, bulk and mass.

They say the keratin parts of us make
fine medicine. Tumours will melt,
warts disappear into little pink circles

on the skin. Hair will be resurrected
like retreads. Passion will debouch
from every pore. Our tongues are charms

against death. Of course we cannot benefit
from such medicine ourselves. Cannibalism
is anathema to us. So are bad manners.

Bless us, if you will, in the time of the dry savannah
and the summer rains. Our carcasses are ships
navigating the storms of carrion, maggots, flies.

GAIL DENDY

Suitcase

Unburdening myself, I pack away last week's
cloudburst, a plastic sheep, five years of hell
at high school, my first, bumbling kiss,

the grandparents I never met, the scent
of bath oil spilt on the mat, a new-born kitten,
raisin bread, mielie kernels. And, of course,

myself as I will be in my dotage, since
the suitcase can expand to hold it all.
Lastly, I shall leave it at the station

without a label or a ticket, already
at its destination, waiting for the stranger
who will pick it up, treasure it, go on living.

GAIL DENDY

Whisker

A single cat's whisker
has been left,
a tiny trembling white line
dropped onto the carpet.
My daughter, three years old,
rubs it between thumb and forefinger
and holds it up
               to the light.

She can obviously handle
what I cannot, its tensile beauty,
its tapering fishing-rod form,
its pale-to-darkening root,
the itch or twitch
that lets it go.

      For the cat, it's a small lost part
of the means of divination
of space and breadth.

      For my daughter, it's something
to put in her special paint box,
or to forget about.

      For me, it's the humming, buzzing
antenna we all must discover
sooner or later, persistent as
         the burnt-out wisp

of a firecracker on New Year's Eve,
a moment irrevocably gone,
	marking whatever arrives.

                GAIL DENDY

The survival kit

There has been a flood.
Everything that the child eats
seems to taste like snow
dripping like aloe sap.
Secrets can be earth-shattering.
Humanity is not meant
To keep secrets. Secrets can kill.
So their bodies flowed
with the water's carcass.

    ABIGAIL GEORGE

Koorsboom

Groen op groen op groen
waar Tukkies se Skip
langs die koorsboompark
voor anker staan

by 'n speelgroepie in Pierre van Ryneveld
is 'n ou grote afgekap oor
sy dorings die ouers
slapelose nagte besorg het

'n kindertekening van *Acacia xanthophloea*

skemertyd gaan stap ons saam
langs Ngwenya Lodge se koorsboomlaan
jy wys die swart ontgiftingstakke uit
hoe slim, gesofistikeerd is dié mooi bome nie

wortels wat méér lewe gee

hoog bo
Breedestraat Erasmuskloof
hou sy 'n voëlnes tussen haar dorings vas
soos in 'n krokodilwyfie se bek

Dis koud. Ek stap met 'n flits
om te kyk:
rol sy regtig haar blaartjies
op in die nag?

SUNELLE GEYER

Fever tree

Green upon green upon green
where next to the park with fever trees
Tuks' Ship
stands at anchor

at a playgroup in Pierre van Ryneveld
an old, large one had been chopped down
because its thorns
gave parents sleepless nights

a child's drawing of *Acacia xanthophloea*

at dusk we walk together
along Ngwenya Lodge's lane of fever trees
you point out the black detoxifying branches
how clever, sophisticated these beautiful trees are

roots giving yet more life

high above
Breedestraat Erasmuskloof
she cradles a bird's nest between her thorns
like in the jaws of a female crocodile

It's cold. I'm walking with a flash-light
to go see:
does she really roll up her tiny leaves
at night?

SUNELLE GEYER
Translated by Johann de Lange

Ma says

Ma says the kittens will live;
it cost too much
but it's worth the pleasure.
Small things, she says, small things.

She rings to tell me she dreamt of death,
of reaching the other shore.
And when she woke she found she was
praying but now she's not sure for whom.

Her mouth is sore,
do I know what they've done?
Taken bone from her hip
for her jaw.

Really at this age
you've seen too much,
she says, too little
is left to be done.

But when can I come?
she asks me again,
because I live so far
now, she says.

And also, Ma says,
she can't quite remember
the smell of my skin
like she used to.

CHANTELLE GRAY

All the Men

Let's say I left the office at that hour
the sun catching me unsunglassed so I squint
against the light slicing off mirrored windows.

Let's say I was on my phone but no-one
was taking my call and I felt life settle
around me like a black cloak soaked
in formaldehyde and mould.

Let's say someone I don't know
smiled and mouthed hello –

his hair falling like a curtain
across his face, a cigarette
curling smoke from the corner of his mouth.

Let's say his eyes were like pools
of dirty oil on water.

Let's say he asks if we've met before.

Let's say I know his unshaven chin and that
his hands will be warm and when we kiss
he'll bite my lip. I know that forest-cat walk.
I know that idle smile.

Let's say soon I'll be staring at myself
in the mirror pinching my waist, my belly
wondering what he sees,
waiting for his telephone call.

Let's say the last time he fucks me
will be on a cold stone floor, while outside
the sun will be sinking into a darkened horizon.

> KERRY HAMMERTON

The Moment

They finally learnt to be rebels
in their thirties – fresh tattoos and
belly rings. She stayed an extra week
just to be part of the recklessness, the wine,
the laughter around the table.
Long evening walks
on the beach to cool their feet,
sun-tanning on the balcony
and making promises to no-one.

She can never untangle each memory,
find the exact moment her son
was conceived: the house torn down now,
a nightclub in the cinema, the tidal
pool washed away by storms and
waves, the beach narrowed and
inaccessible. *I wanted it to go on
forever*, she thinks, *for us to be
forever almost grown-up
yet never growing up.*

KERRY HAMMERTON

water rising

                                                         wind

                            today

  (trees skeletal

          horizontal)

                  rain

        yesterday more

(street lamps

          tilted)

                            (buildings concealed)

                across the land

                      mist

        fog

settling

(stars blank)

                                       expected

(people injured

        dying)

                          hail

            on sunday

(earth washed away)

       sleet

                     snow

                     forecast

          (clouds grey)

                     snow

              forecast

          (sky black)

(water rising)

            KERRY HAMMERTON

Politics in Parliament

The Tree near the window makes a shadowed wall
High leaves are birds
Low leaves fall
A hole frames glass
Hard, open to our sky,
Light comes and goes in green (and red),
And – by the by – inside,
A President speaks,
But these buildings stand on rusting leaves

VERNON R.L. HEAD

The limited attractions of Australia for the elderly and the dead

A friend's mother wants to emigrate to Australia.
Or so she says. Her oldest son
the one who isn't gay, lives there.

Or should I put it like this: she is 87
and lives alone in a flat with a view of the sea.
Her adult children are worried about her.

Her oldest son and his family live in Australia
in a large house, there is plenty of room for her.
She says she want to emigrate

but her husband (their father) is buried here,
how can she leave him, at this late stage?
And go to Australia?

Her husband never even visited Australia
while he was alive.

I see her point.

COLLEEN HIGGS

Animals are the evidence

An Orca shows up in Nootka Sound
Newfoundland, and stays
four years. Everyone has a theory.
Nobody knows why.

This is not a poem about a whale.
This is a poem about the transience
of truth. It is about knowledge and
its passing. It is about how we treat
dead ideas with amnesia, how we're
hooked by the next fabrication.
This is a poem about stupidity.

This is a poem that circles
in the grass like a dog
before lying down. It is
a poem that says nothing
because we still don't understand
a thing. Animals are the
evidence.

An Orca shows up in Nootka Sound
Newfoundland, and collides
four years later with a tugboat.
The Orca's name
is Luna, or L98. The first people
call him Tzuux'iit.

The tugboat's name
is General Jackson.

Everyone has a theory.
Nobody knows why.

    SANDRA HILL

Love in the time of extinction
– a found poem –*

Love is complex. Full of problems
A tree strung with the strange fruit
of cruelty. A growing cascade of extinctions
caused by a single species. Namely our own.
It is a fact of death. The war dogs are us.

I really only want to say we can love
and still be dangerous. For we are
rain dogs too – unable to recognise
everyone and everything as both
Other and Beloved, no longer knowing
how to find our way home. Face-to-face.

SANDRA HILL

---

* Dobrah Bird Rose. *Wild Dog Dreaming: Love and Extinction.* University of Virginia Press, Charlottesville, 2011

Beautiful

And at the end
With nothing left
But weeping men
And damaged souls,
I found, at last,
Beauty there
And sweet perfection
Disguised as Death.

ROCHELLE JACOBS

Dear Dad

You always loved the one
With the broken wings.
Convinced you could teach her to fly.
Wanting to, needing to, make it all alright.

You always loved the one
With the broken wings.
And I guess she got that right:
She pulled herself together
And tore herself apart.

I don't know how, I failed somehow;
I pulled myself together
Pulled and pulled until it stuck
Held in one piece with cellotape
And dried up chewing gum.

And even then, that fell apart:
I broke inside and tried to
Pretend. Pretend and pretend
That your anything-but-love
Could save me from myself.

You always loved the one
With the broken wings.
My wings were fine.
My wings were glued down.

I was put-together-perfect
And you couldn't love me anyway.

    ROCHELLE JACOBS

Something Other

I am not
Any one thing
And I am not nothing.
I am not broken
Or fixed but I
Still need some fixing.
I am not brave or
A coward, angry or sad
And I am not
Going to lie, I am not
Much to look at.
I am not very clever
And I am not stupid either.
I am not at all guilty
But I am damn well ashamed.

All I want is to be something –
Any one thing –
Make me anything
That's different from nothing;
To be something and feel
Like that is ok.
I don't care if it's angry
Or sad or forgiving. All I want
Is to be something,
Not defined by that One Thing
You did to me that day.
I know I could be something –

Even the guilty are that one thing –
And I know that I'm not guilty
So why am I ashamed?

ROCHELLE JACOBS

Children Watching Old People

malume* drinks
the last of his chibuku beer
as though he were
knocking out
bone marrow,
hitting the carton
      violently
against the
palm of his hand
& licking
      the score
noisily.

         THABO JIJANA

---

* *Malume* means uncle in isiXhosa.

Grandma's People

A good example of someone
who sleeps very well
after doing inappropriate things
all day, every day,
is grandma's rooster
casually climbing down
off a fowl, as if releasing himself
from a handshake
gone longer
than necessary
– he rejoins his gaggle
of his two-legged people
with an unlaboured strut
without an ounce of shame;
I'm done here, he could be saying
– already he would be looking out
for something else to do.

THABO JIJANA

The Thing about Mugabe

young men
in baseball caps
& golf shirts
with fake leather purses
heaved like a bunch
of clown's balloons
on both arms,
hawking
door to door
without any shame;

the township *noxolo*
— on a street
Zimbabwean bagmen
funnel past a shanty
with a rickety postern
& Lucky Dube
at max volume,
the same crooked tree
casting thin shadows
in the vanishing light
of dusk
on the front yard

they pass through life
like orphans & runaways
their days
a prophesy disbelieved
but never forgotten

they cannot
escape
the dirty look

       THABO JIJANA

How does a marriage die?

How does a marriage die?
Well, mine died slowly.
First the teeth fall out.
Well, mine did anyway.
The sharp shearers and big biters that had always fought to feed and fend for me.
I wiggled them around as they came loose, wishing them gone.
I knew he didn't like them.
They only got in the way.

I'm safe now, I said to myself.
Don't think I really need teeth any more.
So, when they finally started crumbling and falling free,
I choked on the pieces while eating the seared tuna dinners he prepared.
And we ate in silence.
I examined the gummy, tender patches in the bathroom mirror.
He barely looked at me and said my breasts were too small.
I would have bitten a man for saying so before,
But I was toothless.
And I believed him.

In the next stage of marital death, the brain melts.
Well, mine did, anyway.
I cooked it slowly.
Silencing its complaints over the heat of countless cigarettes.
I smoked myself brainless as the days dropped to the floor.

I lay in bed and watched TV.
Dead TV.
Brain-dead TV.
Hundreds and hundreds of hours of Jerry Seinfeld's smile
and women having sex in a city somewhere.
Gangsters. Lawyers. Detective dramas bleeding into
forensic investigations.
I inhaled grey smoke and other people's lives.
Anything, anything but the vacuum of my own.

Then my nerves started firing.
An all-day electrocution of anxiety and sparks.
Nights wide-awake on the lip of a black hole.
In the middle of the bed.
A canyon.
A cleft.
I woke up alone.
I walked alone.
I crossed the road behind him as he strode silently ahead.
I bit my nails.
I cut off my hair.
I shook in the silence of Saturday afternoons.

It's a bit like drowning, which is the part that comes next.
Drowning in scorn.
His scorn.
His scorn.
Seeping up wetly in waves from the earth.
You talk too much.
You're too serious.

Why don't you paint your toenails?
Why don't you laugh more?
Why do you turn out your feet when you walk?
It turns me off.
I hate your mother.

After a while I stopped fighting the tide.
Just floated on it.
Floated, then sank.
Sank down until my fingers turned to bluish prunes.
Why bother?
Why bother swimming when there's only water in sight?

The last stage is sleeping sickness,
A final retreat into sleep and sleep.
It's a sad, deep-breathing creep.
A comforting drift that inches you closer to the death
that's already upon you.
Sigh. Yes. Please.
Truth be told, he slept more than me towards the end.
He probably felt the pending passing too.
Must have known the very thing he said he didn't want.
That we were both dead and buried already in the bed.
But we played the silly living game a while longer.
Spent hours and hours asleep alongside each other.
Asleep, almost not breathing.
But at least we weren't awake to know and to fight.

Then one day it happened.
It was a Thursday.
I woke up and saw my dead face reflected in a window pane.
My dead teeth piled up in a mound on the floor.
That's funny, I never noticed them before.
But there they were.
So simple, so clear.
And there was my mortality like a rolled-up newspaper that appears suddenly on the doorstep.
My dead fingers drew another cigarette from the box.
My dead brain turned a single word over and over in its pulpy core.
Go.
Go. Go. Go. Go. Go. Go. Go.
It took six months.
But I did.

JUSTINE JOSEPH

Soap

Hair on soap,
Yuck,
She hates it,
That,
dark curly thing that makes her feel unclean,
Like,
A fly in milk,
Like,
regretting,
A mistake.

The condom break,
Fuck!
She hates it,
That,
dark curly thing that happened when she was seventeen,
Like,
spilt milk on the floor,
Then,
scrubbing, scraping,
Her mistake.

But now,
Fifteen years later,
She sees hair on soap,
Sees,
The scrubbing,
Sees,
The mistake.

Then,
She picks it up,
And,
Shrugs a little,
And,
She washes her hands,
And,
Goes on again,
Clean.

   JUSTINE JOSEPH

Kokwana u fambile – Grandmother is gone
(A tribute to Maya Angelou)

The sun crawled
    (*kokwana u fambile*)
The moon howled
    (*u fambile kokwana*)
The stars exploded
    (*kokwana u fambile*)
The forests whispered
    (*u fambile kokwana*)
The rivers sang
    (*kokwana u fambile*)
The oceans moaned
    (*u fambile kokwana*)
The desert blackened
    (*kokwana u fambile*)
The mountains vowed
    (*u fambile kokwana*)
The winds screamed
    (*kokwana u fambile*)
The night crumbled
    (*u fambile kokwana*)
The day broke
    (*kokwana u fambile*)

MOSES NZAMA KHAIZEN

The Spring Rains

What kind of drought is this: that paints all seasons red
Herbert Chitepo, child of Watsomba
Do you find peace still in the quiet of your grave
Amidst the wails and ails of mother Zimbabwe

As she dances violently on the burning coals of lost dreams
Groans are a contained composition of imposed pain
What kind of war is this: fought without end

Gukurahundi: the drizzling early rains of shame
Chaff cannot wash away chaff
The spring rains have long died in the clouds
You have killed the corn and nurtured the weeds
Tsholotsho clothed in the stench of dripping gore of pardoned hatred
Matabeleland is a hidden grave of those despised by angel Gabriel
The divine works of the holy anointed Fifth Brigade
What kind of rain is this: that pours bullets like hail
But the chaff will be washed still, and the fields readied for the plough
What kind of war is this: of brother-sister in self-slaughter

Gukurahundi: the drizzling early rains of hate
The cursed dark cloud lingers on the blue sky still
A ravaged race for piteous remnants
Shona and Ndebele are children of Zimbabwe
ZANLA and ZIPRA are confused memories of defeated victory
ZANU-PF is a decaying forest of hollowed seeds

A crumbling building erected on cursed foundations
Thorns nurtured, and the wheat uprooted
Britain continues still to feed her own amidst insults
Rwanda's brute derives from Zimbabwe's graceful breasts
Only crippled United Nations kept her cool
What kind of war is this: of self-destruction par excellence

Chaff can never wash away chaff
Murambatsvina and *Gukurahundi* are but of the same blood
Mothered by the denied blindness of the angel
But when you bled and sweated for the country
We thought you would share the find of that bitter hunt
Tekere, Nkomo, Tsvangirai hang on a shared cross of sin
MDC an infested nest of angry bees
Unity is but a shaking skeleton without breath
Greed can never lay a brick
The wealth is gone with the shifting oceans
Zimbabwe's children die with degree papers in pockets
What kind of war is this: that shatters the hopes of its people

You spit honey and scatter the bees of your land
Thomas Mapfumo, Oliver Mtukudzi, Alick Macheso
Singing voices echoing love in foreign lands; abandoned children
Babylon has no mercy beloved angel
No life in the tin houses of bulging cities of South Africa
The Methodist Church cannot cough or laugh anymore
Chitepo: your children die in the winter colds of our Johannesburg

A meal for the starving crocodiles of the Limpopo
What kind of mother leaves her own in the desert to fry
Even then, time is a crawling tortoise
In the end, even angels revert to their creator
When a mother decides to be a grave
What kind of war is this: of a soul in quarrel with the self

Gukurahundi: the drizzling early rains of burdened chaff
Brutal rains of pouring death and dry waters
Blunting ululations, condemning dance, breeding sorrow
Zimbabwe crawls in the darkness of blood
Grinding poverty ground as a lasting meal
We thought brigades were for peace and security
What is this journey that never ends
Would a tiger shed its skin: and dance naked for a laughing world
Blood and sweat do not coin flowery dreams
Chitepo: The mat in your grave's floor must be in tatters
And the peace of your sleep stolen
Perhaps, perhaps you should not worry
For we buried death the day you died in your car

MOSES NZAMA KHAIZEN

13 December 2013

I

After twenty frantic years
we line Nelson Mandela Drive,
stilled.

I catch a glimpse of purple between tree leaves.
Alice Walker would be proud.
I hear a chopper overhead –
women more mindful than I,
ululate
as a hearse whizzes past.

How foolish of me
to expect soldiers and brass brands.

He is Free –
from us,
from gushing celebrities
(and models looking for honorary grandfathers),
from requests embossed on glossy paper,
from ruptured relations.

Out pours
twenty years
of buried grief.

II

I am Free.

I escaped the unfreedom
that persists in the streets
of my village.

The price of escape:

the smell of the earth
after the thunderstorm.

the interminable squabble
with proud weeds
pushing through cracks in the veranda,
asserting their right to be.

the birds at home
in the mulberry tree.

mulberries
red to blue-black
falling over pitch-black soil.

silence…
you haven't heard a bird sing
or the roar of a car engine,
until heard against that quality of silence.

III

Lives I left behind:

Dikeledi – her big, open face
at its best, radiant –
then slowly, slowly,
too slowly –
Aids took over.

Thabo – my first best friend –
my first male friend –
rape and robbery hung over his head –
before death ended his terror.

It's hard to say
when Thabo ended,
and the monster began.

Tshepiso - dark beauty
who met the kind of poverty,
that drives a mother
to sit with her children
around a small table
in a rented room
that she could no longer afford
for the last meal
whose poison will burn their insides
and Free them forever.

IV

I have tears for Madiba.

For
Thabo
Tshepiso
Dikeledi,
there is a fury
that scorches tear ducts
dry.

GERTRUDE TRUDI MAKHAYA

Misfathered

I

When you talk about him
your bewildered eyes
half-smile
soft voice
tell me that there was love

He thought he was his own man
until the day came
when moving trucks stood outside
(a rare dignity for a black man)
to relocate you
in line with the master plan

His love's impotence
drove him into shadows
of his choice

II

Misfathered
you mistrust love

You choose to stand alone

Unfathered
I carry on

III

I am water
each step I take
up the clinic's stairs
I feel in my bloated belly

In the bleak theatre
anonymised by a blue gown
into yet another woman whose silver strands
came before motherhood
I am carried off into nothingness

To wake up to a cold salad
then legal formalities
before I am free
to suspend the future

twelve oocytes
to be frozen
to be fathered

GERTRUDE TRUDI MAKHAYA

Semputšiše

Ke malibilibi matolo-masehlana
Ema thabeng o goeletše magalagapa palega
Ke bona dipônô
Ke nkadingala ditorong ke ntšhotšhonono

Ba re bantoile
Ke re bantoile
Bamphile ka ja ka sohla
Ke lesegafela
Lenaba la meetse seilakatse

Ngwana llela nakana
Ya mokhura ba mphile
Mpholo wona diabolo o nngwathetše
Ya ba go ntaletša sinagogeng ya lefsifsi
Molete-mohlaelathupa

Ke khupamarama bjang ke sepela ke hlobotše?
Ke dijo mang dilewa ke bafsa feela?
Ke koma mang e sa alogeng?
Nyaope o tšhiwana ya ga mang?
O thuri-mang re go phase wa badimo?

                    KATISE MAWELA

Don't Ask Me

It's a torn clothes it's pale legs
Stand on a mountain top and shout out loud
I see visions
I am a traditional healer I am a giant

They say they bewitched me
I say they bewitched me
They filled my stomach with food
I laugh for no reason
I detest bathing I hate cats

I wanted more responsibility
They gave me
The devil gave me his portion of poison
As an invitation to his synagogue of darkness
The grave

How am I a secret when I walk around naked?
What food am I that gets eaten by youth only?
What initiation am I that has no graduation?
Whose orphan are you; drugs?
What gnome are you not to be appeased like ancestors?

KATISE MAWELA
Translated by Goodenough Mashego

rough draft

the waste water was running
in small channels along the street
as it does all year round, in
alex

a thin dog
warmed itself in the fabulous, flimsy, feeble morning sun
a mutt without the cares
of a suburban dog

a child comes by
with play in her eyes
& a piece of bread in hand
a girl, in school uniform
stepping carefully to avoid the muck

a foreign friend diego is with me
he sings a portuguese song
as we amble down third avenue

he speaks of a crucible for deep conversation
he speaks of
the alchemy of social change & memory work

one day before the fifth elections
i went to alex
early in the morning
and he came with
camera hanging from his shoulder

FRANK MEINTJIES

Letter from Marikana

Oko ndazalwa.
Uthando olunje,kangaka
andilwazi
nditsh'ukuba ke bhelukazi ndiyakuthanda.
Yaye Ndiyakukhumbula

ayoma amathe ndithetha ngawe
iyabaleka intliziyo xa ndikucinga.
Namathandabuzo ayaphela kulemfazwe yethu nabacinezeli
ingoma imilambo ndilinde usuku lwethu apho ndizakuba
ngumyeni wakho
izale iphuphume imilambo zinyembezi ndikulilela
kulentlupheko yase Marikana
nob'ungaphum'umphefumlo egameni lokulwela ubomi
bethu bubengcono
ndiza kuxhwarha emasangweni wezulu
ndikulindile ngomonde wena bomikazi bam.

Ndeza apha ndisithi ndizela ukusebenzela ikamva lethu.
Xola uba ndingekathumelinto
Sisagwayimba
Abelungu abafuni nemali kodwa siyayimba
Unike unyana wethu uthando nakum iyasik'inimba
Kodwa inkokheli yethu ithi siqhube nemfazw'ekugqibeleni
bazakusiva.

Iinkumbulo zam ngathi zigxininisa ubukho bomdali
phakathi kwethu
kuba ithemba lingaphakathi esifubeni
ibhotwe lakho mnt'omhle
kule imbalela nguwe amanzi...

Sizakuyifumana iR12 500
Ndikulobole ukwehla kwam ngoDisemba...
Le ndandiyiphumele apho elalini ibe ifeziwe
Njangesivumelwano sethu sizakubuya ndizokunisebenzela
wena nonkwenkwe
Unyana wethu.

Oh kodwa kubuhlungu okwangoku
Kodwa ndiqiniswa ngamazwi akho xa usithi
"yonk'int'izoba right...Yomelela"
Ndibulela umdali ngokubeka intliziyo yam ezandleni
zakho ezishushu
Ndilala ndivuka ndiphupha olo suku uzakube usesifubani sam.
Aliqela amabali endizakubalisela sakubonana
Kodwa khawube usomelela ukhumbule iminqophiso yethu
koluthando

KOMISA MFINGO

Letter from Marikana

Since I was born
I've never known love like this
Today I love and remember you

My saliva dries up talking of you
I lose my mind thinking of you
Even gossip is irrelevant in this fight we have with
oppressors
I wait in song for our day
When I shall be your bride
I shall be teary with excitement
I cry for you due to the Marikana disaster
Before you lose your soul
For a fight for a better life
I will rush to the gates of heaven
And wait for you my love

I come here to work for our future
Forgive me for not sending anything
We are still on strike
The whites don't want to pay but we are hopeful
Give my regards to your child
Our leader says we must hold on
At the end our cries will be heard

My thoughts strengthen the bond our creator gave us
Hope resides in my heart
Your pot beautiful one
Is the source of my water…

We will get the R12 500
Marry you when I come down in December
Take you to church and make it official
We will fulfil our agreement
I will work for you and our child
Our child

Today it's painful
I draw strength from your words when you say;
"everything will be alright… Stay strong"
I thank the lord for putting my heart
In your warm hands
I sleep wake up and dream that day that
You will lie on my chest
Stay strong and remember
Our promise of everlasting love

KOMISA MFINGO
Translated by Goodenough Mashego

i know a guy

they hung his grandfather by the feet
built a fire underneath
and cooked him

fuck them, he says
i hate them, broke one of their legs one day
fuck them

and who
can argue

humanity: our greatest illusion

we kill
we burn

they do too

in forests and office blocks
wrapped in ties, smothered with dirty, stinking old shoes

they kill
they burn

and we do too

ANDREW MILLER

Devil's Fish

What we brought back, what we brought from dark waters
Was nothing you could brag of, nothing you could weigh
Or mount above a desk. We just hooked some words
That'll always stick. Like bitch. Like whore
No one remembers what for. Just one day we were slipped
Or tipped slowly out into the dark glass,

And came up flapping blood. Thing is we got too mad
To pull the hook out. (Oh to pull it back till
The bones crack, before it's out!) Got to like the cold
Silence and the to and fro of the sea's leaning
To gently unhook our souls
From the stitches of our bones.

We are the chewed blue sack that wells to light
As something found. Its words we bring
Back, what they dragged from us, blue,
Dragged sweet roses, dragged right through
The world of what we knew, to this palace of tears,
The sweet waters of letting go.

A hundred fish have carried off the secret
Of our hearts and the last place we set our eyes.
Our mothers have forgotten we were ever alive,
They're in other rooms we will never arrive
(Our skins are white as weddings
They lay their eggs in us like pearls)

We are the devil's fish,
We never stay where we are bundled
And weighted with stones.
We fish the hearts that drowned us
On the hooks of our dreaming. We sing
Songs of sorrow to the white eye of the moon.

                JANINE JOCELYN MILNE

Eulogy

Here she comes, the pigeon bride!
Her train is tar and as speckled with white
As a bronze horse in a park! The gum is borrowed
And the maids in matching grey
Knit with twine and twisted toes
A bouquet of feathers and vegetable rinds.

And boy is she blue, now that she's flown
The coop. Wasn't much to lose
But her dirty crew, shrugging lice like rice,
See the world turn as dark as an eagle's shade
At her pass. [They promise to wait each day
Where they saw her last.]

They are all there. To take her piece by piece
To where they fly. She shines now
As yellow as the stains on her fingers.
Saint of the rollups, queen of the street
Sacred heart of her grey feathered flock
Rising from her loneliness. Complete.

[Even the sun that lost its toes long ago
And cannot land, has climbed up high
To pour bright blessing on the wedding
With tattered yellow wings.]

What a dirty feast no one has thrown!
There's carrot tops and potato peel
Under her rising feet and stale bread flows
From her fingers and her toes!
There's not a dry eye on the block
[Even though she is buried alone].

Birdsong breaks the sky with her name
And carries her up, up, over the pain
Of her thin bones. A million gravel throats sing
Of such Sadness in her name, that Jesus himself
Looks to her with love, from the side of his eye,
And feeds her crumbs from under his wing.

     JANINE JOCELYN MILNE

Train

Morning hangs back outside the hiss snick
of the doors. I pretend to be blind as I feel for a space
between eyes

and settle in a *thug life* hanging off the grey
slick seat. Angry men have left their signs – an apocalypse
of felt tip pens.

The council has stitched up their victims, thick fingered,
an autopsy of sick blue seats. In the K tik K tak K tik
head's bob on cut strings.

I don't know why the dead ride the trains
while the scarred walls fling trees again and again
against the windows

they mouth the air,
their faces nod, as white against the glass
as babies in formaldehyde jars

their leaning in too much to bear.
Pigeons with crippled feet keep the tracks from spilling in.

but they do. Newlands-Mowbray-Salt River-Cape Town
like yellow beads on a rosary they pray

in rust and splinters. Under-
the beast metal is singing the earth to scraps.

JANINE JOCELYN MILNE

Kankere, o selo mang?

O maru a se nang tladi malebatsa
Letsele le re le antseng masi a botshelo
Le tswa lengope le le botlhole ba loso
Fela jaaka moloi, ga o mmala

O tsena ka tidimalo e e tsenelletseng
Re tshoga kgwethe mo letseleng
Tshega e fapogile metsetelo
Bosula ba gago bo setse bo ile magoletsa

O tlhasela mmele o sa kgetholle
O tsenella marapo o a je mmoko
Boidiidi ba go ata ga gago bo a boitshega
O le mmitsa-ntšwa o o sa tsholang thupa

O ikala medi jaaka setlhare mo nokeng
Makala a gago a gagola le sebete tota
Botlhoko ba gago bo se na bokhutlo
Masetlapelo e le bogobe ba rona ba malatsi otlhe

O selo mang wena o sa bonweng
Fa sekhukhuni se bonwa ke sebataladi
Le baitseanape tota ba retelelwa ke pheko
Ditlhong e se sepe, o tshegisa ka tsholofelo ya rona

O nole Mme botshelo go fitlhela lerothoding la bofelo
Botshelo ba gagwe bo nyelelela re ntse re lebile
Maano re a logile ga sita a loso
Bokhutlong a raga thokolo, a neela moa

Legale mo losong Mme o bone boikhutso bo bo sa khutleng
Selo ke wena ga o kitla o ikhutsa le e seng
Sa gago ke go tlalatlala naga, o sasanka bosigo le motshegare
O tsoma motswasetlhabelo yo o latelang.

JACKIE MONDI

Cancer, what the hell are you?

Your entrance causes no stir
The breast from which we suckled lifegiving milk
Grows a malignant lump that leads to death
As you make an inconspicuous entrance

You come in deep silence
While we reel in the shock of the lump
It is too late
As your evil is now widespread

You attack the body indiscriminately
Crunching the bones down to the marrow
Your boundless spread is fearsome
You do your harm unseen

You spread your roots like a tree by the river
Your branches tearing even the liver apart
Your devastation unending
Pain, our daily bread

If everything comes to light eventually
What the hell are you that you cannot be seen
Even scientists cannot find a cure
You have made a mockery of our hope

You sucked the life out of her even to the last drop
Our mother's life vanishing in front of our eyes
Our tactics to save her life stopped at death's door
Finally she gave in and gave her last breath

Even so in death mother received eternal rest
And you damned thing will never find rest
Your lot is to roam the earth, wandering day and night
Searching for your next victim.

JACKIE MONDI
Translated by Jackie Mondi

Scenes from India I – Beautiful

The first thing I noticed was her hair.

It was riding the wind, flapping like a delicate black sari on a washing line. She never made a single move to pull its current back; she just let it run like an inky trail out of the back of the six-seater. Her face sat like a baked clay globe in her mass of hair – a torch shining through a thicket.

I felt bad that my frame consumed so much of the seat. Her hip bone lodged itself tightly against the flesh of my right buttock.

The kind of pain you like.

But if I hadn't tied her down so tightly, she would have been swept away by the river of her hair. It made me feel helpful – necessary even – a rock tied to the end of a wayward balloon.

Then her *doopatha** dropped.

A shivered in the presence of her naked shoulder. Her left hand ran in search of the scarf's damson tail. She hurriedly flung it over her shoulder again and accidentally flicked my nose.

The kind of pain you like.

---

* The scarf Indian women wear over their *salwar kameez* as part of their daily attire.

Her fingers came so close that I could smell a bouquet of dust and sweat. I knew that she must have touched all kinds of things: taps, railings, doorframes, desks, chairs, cups and then … my nose. She had a life outside this vehicle: a busy one.

I had nothing of the sort to offer her.

But now – *this* girl – she touches my nose … and then nothing. She doesn't flinch. No "mojhe moaf karo,"* or shy-embarrassed eyes. Nothing.

The tip of my nose was not worth acknowledging.

I resolved to stare at her bumping breasts as the vehicle dipped in and out of the potholes. I wanted to scan the crude valleys around her eyes and lips but she hid behind her hair and her *doopatha*. That frothy-cloth – a hideous purple – like dead blood collected underneath a bruise. We made it all the way to the station and I never really saw her face.

Maybe it was better that way.

What if she had really been beautiful?

I couldn't handle that.

NEDINE MOONSAMY

---

* "I'm very sorry"

Scenes from India II – A walk into the Park

The sun hung above like a torch: direct and professional in purpose.
The heat was hungry and it licked ten antecubitals, ten helixes, five napes.
The Asphalt path stretched forward like a long black tongue,
five heads drooped like bent spoons,
ten feet dipped into each of its gravel pores.
Bearing traces of sweat and dust,
ten thighs felt the chafing of a wet rust.

The Park was a balmy oasis.
It sucked them in through green and leafy lips.
Ten eyes watched as lovers sat in pairs, building conspiratorial memories
that time we skipped class and hid in the park and spoke for hours.
Like proverbial Adams and proverbial Eves, they sought coverage amongst the foliage.
Carvings on the trees told other stories
Anul was here.
The makeshift piles of discarded sweet wrappers whispered their tastes
Baballo and Munch.

But further in, the Park abandoned them.
The leaves became too varied, the branches too entangled, the flowers too hybrid to know.

Five minds strained against the unkempt earth:
1) Too ignorant to enjoy analytically.
2) Too cynical to enjoy romantically.
3) Too clique to enjoy poetically.
4) Too consumerist to enjoy individually.
5) Too urban to enjoy pastorally.

A fitting entry for Silence to arrive.
But she is elusive.
A butterfly you catch and let go of out of guilt.

"Oh, look at that, isn't it beautiful!" He remarked.

NEDINE MOONSAMY

Circumference, Lion's Head

EAST, 100M
Silver city, drifting mist, the golden bay alight.
The Helderberg blue beyond, draped in banks
of cloud; purple, pink, peach-cheeked aurora,
lapping apices in mist and light.
The buildings imposed in silhouette,
sprinkled between the hills: the looming
scaffolds of the harbour, the apartments
creeping up the slope. Closer, sentinel
groups of red-streaked rocks, the last
flowers in bloom, peeking magenta and yellow.
I look to the peak. I take the dirt path upward.

SOUTH, 270M
"That looks a bit of a challenge."
A British couple sits on a bench, talking about
the distant gorge opposite, creeping
up the side of Table Mountain. The man
zigzags his hand in mime through the cleft,
divining the rock, the water running in the gorge;
the woman bends over and sighs.

WEST, 520M
Dots of white houses glint in the bay below.
I grip the chains and haul myself up the cliff.
I spot a narrow-billed bird trilling, perched
on a protea, looming pink and white above.
I look down to the ocean, the crashing
sea foam, the dull vastness of it. This,
I think, hanging under birdsong, is not my domain.

NORTH, 669M

The summit, somehow, wind-coarse and clear. I walk
to the plateau's furthest edge, spot the merchant ships
circling Robben Island; the coral clumps of fynbos
underfoot. The sun begins to break through.
The city hums, its shouts sanded down to simple grain:
the wholeness of it – the years, the vice, the quotidian
dread – taken in one glance; the slow porcelain
roll of days; brittle and vacant and far.

NICK MULGREW

a June missive

The day your father died I was in Fulham. I
remember that because it was something that
mattered to me then. My brother was married that

morning in the town hall. Afterwards I sent a message
to you in Blouberg. I remember you didn't reply. It's
something I can't blame you for, obviously – it

was a tough time for you; I think it was for me
too. I felt awash in life that day. I remember walking
drunk down Kensington High Street at midnight in

the suit I had been confirmed in. I'd taken the
wrong night bus from Baron's Court. I tried to
change direction at stops that were alight-only.

I sat in a shelter. For a while a fox sat
in front of me, then yelped and jumped over
a wall before I could take a photo of it.

Where was I in this world? This was a question I
knew everyone asked at some point. I'd like to tell
you I now have an answer, but I don't. I want to say

the lights were bright then but they weren't. I want
to say that I remember all of this in the finest
detail but I don't; I want to tell you I realised

something about myself that day but really I can't.
I want to tell you that you weren't as alone that day
as you perhaps thought you were (although I can't

be sure of that because I am not you and that is for
the better) and this is something I would want to say,
for comfort or otherwise – but I'm afraid it's not true:
you were alone as I was.

NICK MULGREW

'n meisie wat in haar kamer dans

koue koffie vibreer bruin ringe
teen die kant van 'n koppie
lankal reeds vergete
nes die stilte
wat deur note grofgeskut vergruis is
agter die deur van haar enkelkamer
wat in 'n *club scene* omskep is
die bed is haar dansvloer
daar is posters teen die mure
as die musiek tref
resoneer haar hele wese
sy dans op studietafels saam stoele
wat hul vererg as hulle lus word
en sy sit hulle weer neer
die vuil tupperware en kitsch glase
se hakke klik klak klik verbete saam
en die neonlig se oë flikker alweer
as hy te hoog saam swaai
sy headbang graag
gooi haar arms vreesloos in die lig
heeltemal te dronk gedraai
as sy neerstort en lag,
doodnugter op haar bed
terwyl sy lê
en vir die volgende refrein
van vryheid wag.

EDUAN NAUDÉ

a girl dancing in her room

cold coffee vibrates brown rings
along the inside of a cup
long forgotten
just like the silence
shattered by heavy artillery sounds
behind her single bedroom door
transformed into a club scene
the bed is her dance floor
posters adorn the walls
when the music hits
her entire being resonates
she dances on study tables joined by the chairs
that take offence when they catch the groove
and she puts them down again
the heels of the dirty tupperware and kitsch glasses
click clack click along in earnest
and the eye of the neon light flickers once more
as it swings along too high
she likes to headbang
flinging her arms fearless into the air
too drunk from spinning
as she tumbles down sober
on her bed, laughing
waiting for the next
chorus of freedom.

EDUAN NAUDÉ
Translated by Johann de Lange

Bushbaby

It's his first visit.
Mocha-soft skin and tangled curls,
this miniature Mowgli who,
with the wisdom of two
sees no need for clothes.
Feral child.
He disrupts ant-streams
and challenges fat geckos.
"Yook I a yion," he roars.
But when the warthogs
move towards the house,
his kalamata eyes grow wide.
I scoop him up and he holds on tight.

            PAM NEWHAM

Mother in a glass with ice

I remember you.
Mother at the window
waiting to wind your arms around
your child returned from school.

I remember you.
Mother in a glass with ice
late night voices
splintering dreams.
haphazard slurred words
hitting their mark.

I remember you.
Mother in a frail-care bed
silent while your only child
winds you in her arms.

                PAM NEWHAM

Pistachios

Cyprus airport one a.m.
Two women waiting for a flight.
Around us suntanned holidaymakers
stretch out on metal benches
as a tinny voice announces again
our flight has been delayed.

Two dark-eyed boys with stubble chins
want to buy us red wine.
We say no but they tell us
They are Iranians no one wants
and have been in transit for days.
So we let them buy us wine
and when they come back
they pile pistachios on the table.

They tell us they are taxi drivers
and we pretend to believe
their wild tales and they
pretend to be shocked
when they hear
they are half our age.
We laugh and flirt tasting
the saltiness of the pistachios
and the roughness of the wine
until finally they call our flight
and we hug like old friends
or maybe lovers.

An unexpected adventure
So many years ago and yet
whenever I slide my nail between
the slick shell and crack open
a pistachio I recall a hot night
and boys nobody wanted.

            PAM NEWHAM

Please stop the music

A lot of souls are missing in this house
Music is too loud
How do we dance to jazz
When don't get the blues
In songs like senzeni na
Songs composed by passions and tears
Built on top of iNkandla and unrested souls
20 years into democracy we still sing these melodies
But we mute the blues
Up the tempo
And the increase the volume

Please stop the music
The dance floor has too much swag
For 44-year-old Mr Masondo
Whose young heart has left broken hearts and starving bellies
In corridors of aching wombs and abandoned childhoods
They say it takes a nation to raise a child
But how can this man of a house
Seduce his daughter's friend into burying her dreams
In clubs and Brazilian weaves

Please stop the music
The night is packed with DJs, fashion, promiscuity and credit cards
But when morning comes in her humble real-like dress
Our bodies will need doctors, husbands and wives
This country will need a president

And someone has to put a plate of hope and love on
someone's table

Please stop the music
Make sure hip hop is turned off
Because his rhyme speaks of currency
With no culture of saving its soul

Please stop the music
Run your fingers through thick books
Cook
Have a conversation with friends
Sit down
Ponder on the difference of flesh
Find answers to the blues
And compose a new song
But in the meantime
Please stop the music
A lot of souls are missing in this house
Music is too loud

SIZAKELE NKOSI

Xenophobic Society

One of many black brothers in Africa,
Terrorised with rattling guns and petrol bombs,
He fled his country, to live in exile,
Upon foreign land with abundant treasures,
Working underground in a diamond mine,
For the sake of his two beloved children,
Wearing oily tainted grey overalls,

A cold wind blows as the red sun sets,
Dragging his worn out feet on a rocky gravel road,
The way back home is agonisingly distant,
Not far in the mist, a squadron of vicious men,
Wait to pounce on him, like a hungry wolf pack,
They say, "Here he comes, that Makwere-Kwere,"
Silver knives are drawn and long iron pangas,

Disorder erupts when he makes eye contact,
Falling in the trap of a xenophobic society,
He runs left then right, but there's no way out,
The dogs scatter around him, gnawing their sharp teeth,
"Kill the bastard," they jubilantly say,
My brother from another mother, burnt in flames that day
All because he was Zimbabwean.

LAZOLA PAMBO

The Heartbeat
(At Madiba's Funeral)

Captain's heart is still strange:
It beats as always, though his body is cold,
Now long cold.

As Captain's heart continues its beat,
Many are baffled but gain vigour, much
As before
His body grew motionless
And lay still.

Many called it an epoch when,
Through turbulent seas and marauding pirates,
His battered ship touched many shores –
Bringing things of value,
Prized since time began.

And now kings from distant lands
Have come to his.
They have gathered to salute his silent form
As it lies on the deck.
They bring messages and gifts to his people,
But the greatest gift is one they depart with:
That Captain lies dead, yet lives,
That his heart beats strongly still.

                              THABO SESEANE

#6

-please- It's been six days since I saw your skin. I was dog. You were cat. We

were different but why? I hated a rough tongue in my mouth but you held my face on Monday.

-what do you want?- you unhinged my jaw like I was eating your whole liver and each of your plum kidneys.

-here- I said. I was telling you -cut my palms- split them down to ten without tails.

So I showed you my gōngxǐ hands. Again, again when I dried you like gander, rabbit buck and pen.

-could you be any more annoying- I took that down, peeling in my absolution, and fresh like salt, swayed in

place where your chest had been. -I don't like girls, Fran-

FRANCINE SIMON

#8

There is a place in our community we call the fountain.
I meet you there on Thursdays because I only work at three
and we roll ourselves in the water like Cape fur seals.

FRANCINE SIMON

After she is taken home, I watch the news.

Not in their beds,
but on a bare stone floor
they lie in rows – covered,
not tucked in,
by that last white sheet.

Children
just like her,
pale, dark-haired, untouched,
but by the air they breathed,
with long black lashes shut
as if asleep.

Mourned
by grandmothers
just like me.

(News headline:
"Chemical weapons used against civilian population."
Damascus, August 2013)

ANNETTE SNYCKERS

Away

Some days I sit,
sunk like a stone
into the soft seat
of the sofa.
The cat sits next to me
like a sphinx,
eyes screwed into slits.

Only the stone
and the sphinx
stay on the sofa;
we have left the room –
the cat in a trance
of feline fantasy

and I,
I have sailed off
in a ship called Book,
locked in the papery
cabin of its pages.

ANNETTE SNYCKERS

China

Her life is a bone
China cup in a quivering hand
that speaks of England,
clouded in steam,
Darjeeling and Earl Grey.

The half-moon handle is
stuck fast with glue,
but if she were to let go,
her eighty-three-year life
would lie in shards at her feet.

Her granddaughter's life in England
is emerging,
a Starbucks china mug,
dishwasher safe;
Ethiopian and Columbian steam.

If she were to let it slip
through her fingers,
she would leave the pieces and move on.

DIANNE STEWART

The Dancer in Flamenco Strikes

  electing

    quick

clipped

  attack

clocking in with starry whirls firing wheeling lightning turns

stac-

ca

to

        white against the fierce black blistering night

              in electric

                rapid

                spangled

                salvoes

in faultless mirth executing death's horizontal claim

living once in wild control the hearts vast aching hall to fill
to throb to overflow

love's

   rhythm

     ical

  law

    to

 obey

rising strong as the wind above the plain in joy the dancer
fusillades

                                           stamp-

                                            eding

                                         full-

                                           blood-

                                           ed

as the sweating sun by tap and crack on the clamouring planks of Madrid

Los Carboneras

the dancer's blood now coursing in beautiful brutal beat

    the distant applause a brief caress only

        to his naked need of flowering utmost,

            the guitar salute giving out full and slow

                the unbearably sweet last echo

JAN TROMP

Zebra Express

    In the short shade of hot midday
the dry river bed comes alive
      as a strange creature arrives,
         its bold appearance strikes
            down boredom and monotony
it's the bridlebanded darling
      of the African plains
      bright shade horse arrayed by day in fancy dress
as vibrant lightning on the night – zebra express!

    The ochre mountains and midnight blue sky
darkening in the rising storm
      condense in the zebra's spangled flanks
        cantering as a keyboard's
          jazzy melody
        or a black and white movie
          flick-flickering out

the beautiful story

of a life becoming full and free

Fiercely vigilant the zebra drinks

        but danger unseen, more ominous

than the din of thunder overhead

        makes it freeze...

                its nostrils flaring

                      for the cool rain

    s*cent* the lurking predator

        wheeling free from heavydeath for liberty
it runs!

    racing exultant as the rain comes

to a land of promise streaked by the sun

        alive alert in light armour dressed – zebra express!

                                JAN TROMP

adamastor wakes

'Even as I spoke, an immense shape
Materialised in the night air,
Grotesque and of enormous stature,
With heavy jowls, and an unkempt beard,
Scowling from shrunken, hollow eyes,
Its complexion earthy and pale,
Its hair grizzled and matted with clay,
Its mouth coal black, teeth yellow with decay.'

From Luis de Camoes, *The Luciads* (1)

it is uncertain what woke him
the traffic was bad that night
and the people partied on
ringing lampposts like bells
shattering bottles
in wild percussion

the bitch knew alright
she strained at her chains
and hurled herself at the gate
flesh and steel clashing
in a mess of blood and foam

the foghorn moaned
a soft rain fell
but what woke him is uncertain
it could have been the dawn

SUSAN WOODWARD

lights out

unexpected and not exactly welcome
lights out is a gentle unobtrusive guest
arriving suddenly holding her hands over your eyes in a
guess who game
teasing daring you to see the glow in the fridge
or the lightstreaming door of the microwave
if she would but open her fingers

no matter, all is quiet, there is no panic
only a calm groping for the match
the candle your true your faithful friend greets you
with warmth and a soft glow of recognition
and accompanies you to fumble a remembered path to bed
to sleep under stars of ancient times

no it's not lights out that's the problem
it's lights on

GABANG

lights from every room rip through the velvet night
electronic digits flash red in your face
12.00 blip 12.00 blip 12.00 blip
the orchestra of your life starts playing shouting from the
television

oldman refrigerator judders to his tiny feet
monotonemonologuelatenightradiotalkshowvoicedroneson
andonandon

Eskom restores
and you cheer in gratitude

SUSAN WOODWARD

The Captured Maiden

By early sunrise this day
I should have long deserted this place
The spaces far away
In concoction with my people
Have long forgotten the sight of me
Early in the days of my womanhood
I left, in search of your kraal.

Many moons have I counted
The glimmering light consuming
Many by the weary banks of the river pool
Where, as first born of your kraal
I have been master
Of your many ceremonies.

Legions
Long have they deserted you
Big piles of herbs their awards
Crowds behind them
Countless herds scattered
Throughout those sleeping valleys.

Patterning yourself after your predecessors
You suffocated me with your misplaced proverbs
The traditional conclave –
Your main residence
Has lost its relevance.

It is almost a hundred moons now
With me tendering your cattle
And me creating your music
Slouching with your medicinal bag
Over my tattered shoulders.

My defeated husband
Has long forgotten
The warmth of my now tired breasts
I have to please your kindred
With all that I am.

The members of my clan
And those of my traded-in man
Have long been calling me
Through many dreams –
Gushing words from beyond.

With your baboon fly-whisk
And your chameleon head-gear
Have you shrugged their wishes
I could only own
Countless drums of my tears.

Today
I would like you to know
The contents of my last dream
Which I could not pour
Over your stone ears –
To leave you, unseen
For you would never release me.

Have I not paid enough
For the dream that brought me here?
Come, let us dance
For the last time now.

    SITHEMBELE XHENGWANA

Hintsa's Portrait

Through English picturesque, here
he stands. Overburdened with colonial
lexion, he still stands, an intransigent
opponent of colonial advance –

narrative of the war.

Possession of land through
nineteenth century Romantic
imagination – ceded territory.

Here he stands, as a figure
of Xhosa Royality. That only
through political manoeuvring,
Smith could be the true meaning
of a traitor.

Yet, this portrait cannot reflect
the realities of the many voices
still crying for a ceded throne.
Of which the climax was
the burning of Hintsa's kraal
and the mutilation of his body.

And even more, the exportation
of the king's head to the colonial
masters.

        SITHEMBELE XHENGWANA

Biographies

Jim Pascual Agustin writes and translates Filipino and English poetry. He grew up in the Philippines and now lives in Cape Town with his Canadian-born wife and their twin daughters. His fifth and sixth poetry books, *Kalmot ng Pusa sa Tagiliran* (poems in Filipino) and *Sound Before Water*, were simultaneously published in 2013 by the University of Santo Tomas Publishing House in Manila. These books will be followed, in 2015, by a new collection called *A Thousand Eyes*. He is currently at work on two other poetry manuscripts as well as a new project: blending history and poetry from an immigrant's perspective. Read more on his blog: www.matangmanok.wordpress.com.

Kyle Steven Allan is a 27-year-old poet, recording artist, freelance writer, events organiser, and creative all-rounder. He has had poetry published in numerous publications both in South Africa and internationally. He released a multi-genre album of poetry with music titled *Influences*, which has received airplay on various local and national stations. He has contributed columns, features and reviews to publications including *Weekend/Natal Witness*, *Litnet*, *potholesandpadkos* and *Mindmapsa*. He lives in kwaSwayimane, KwaZulu-Natal with his wife Thobeka and son Seymour.

Adewole Armah was born in Qumbu and is currently a student at Rhodes University.

Saaleha Idrees Bamjee is a freelance writer, photographer and incidental designer who lives and works in

Johannesburg. She has an MA in Creative Writing from Rhodes University, Grahamstown. Her story 'Out of the Blue' won the 2014 Writivism Short Story prize in Uganda. Her poetry has appeared in various South African literary journals and is available online at www.saaleha.com.

Suzan-Jane Kathleen Bell is a contemporary South African poet, writer, arts columnist and arts festival curator with an MA in Creative Writing (UCT). She has performed multi-media sonnet re-mixes collaborating with Hilton Schilder on /*xaru*, painted haiku on Wayne Barker's art studio walls, performed prose poetry with DJ Boshoff on psychedelic guitar pedals, and she mixes and blends text with Black South Easter vocalist, Nhoza Sitsholwana. She has performed poetry at the Franschhoek Literary Festival, Badilisha Poetry X-Change Africa Day celebrations, Fire Word Friday's Cape Creative Exhibition, City Breath Festival, contemporary art galleries, night clubs, hotel rooms and independent book shops.

Ayanda Billie is from Uitenhage. She is a freelance writer working at Volkswagen as an operator. In 2006, she published a poetry collection entitled *Avenues of my Soul*. She is currently studying an MA in Creative Writing at Rhodes University.

Fadwah Booley is a borderline recluse from Cape Town who discovered her love for poetry at 14 after reading an article about a boy brutally killed in the Middle East conflict, which inspired her first poem and incessant journal writing. Before heading off to study Science at Stellenbosch University, she ceremoniously burnt this journal and abandoned writing. Her love affair with yoga has been a catalyst for rediscovery of her true self, which allowed her to tune into her innate love for writing. When she's not cultivating her introverted self or tending to cells in the laboratory to pay the bond, she just sits and mind-melds.

Sindiswa Busuku is currently pursuing a Master of Arts at the University of KwaZulu-Natal. She researches and produces creative writing. She is interested in post-memory, or rather, inherited memory, and the ways in which this experience manifests through projection rather than recollection.

Zethu Cakata was born in the Eastern Cape. She started writing poetry when she was 17 years old, but she always hid her work from others. Only when she was much older did she start sharing with close friends. She is a single mother of one and works full-time, writing during her spare time. She has two volumes of poetry and a novel waiting to be published. She hopes to stay at home one day and do nothing else but write. She was raised by reading parents and that ignited her passion for books. She enjoys Xhosa and Nigerian literature such as JJR Jolobe, SEK Mqhayi, Chinua Achebe and Chimamanda Ngozi Adiche, who are her current favourite authors. Her next body of work, after publishing all her current manuscripts, will be in isiXhosa.

Ntyatyi Christian studied Language and Literature at the University of Cape Town as well as at the University of KwaZulu-Natal. She is also a founding member of arts group Keen Artists Theatre, which is presently based at UKZN. She was also one of the original members of the poetry reading circle at the Bat Centre, Izimbongi Zesimanje. Her Honours thesis was a critical reading of the works of various South African poets. She currently works as a copy editor, reviewer and translator.

Margaret Clough grew up in Wellington, Cape Town and has lived in Zambia and George where she worked as a soil chemist and a pyhsical science teacher. She has had poems published in *New Contrast*, *Carapace* and *Aerodrome* and also contributed to the collection *Difficult to Explain* edited by Finuala Dowling. Two of her poems, 'At Least the Duck Survived' and 'The Last to Leave', have been published by Modjaji Books.

Christine Coates has an MA in Creative Writing from the University of Cape Town and is a writer and poet. She also has an interest in life-writing and memoir. Her poems have been published in *New Coin, New Contrast, Carapace, A Hudson Review, Scrutiny2, Deep Water* and *Cambridge Conference of Contemporary Poetry Review: Africa Focus*. Her collection of poetry *Homegrown* will be published by Modjaji Books late in 2014. Her story 'The Cat's Wife' was highly commended recently in the anthology *Adults Only*. She is a member of The Grail Women's Retreat Group as well as Finuala Dowling's monthly poetry group.

Lise Day recently retired to Hout Bay after 40 years of teaching English, most recently at the Nelson Mandela Metropolitan University. She is a member of the Pleached Poetry writing circle and regularly attends workshops with Finuala Dowling. Her short stories have been published in the English National Curriculum text book and in periodicals and books. She has had poems published in *Carapace, The Sol Plaatje European Union Poetry Anthology, New Contrast* and most recently online in *Aerodrome*.

Gail Dendy has published seven collections of poetry, most recently *Closer Than That* (Dye Hard Press) in 2011. She was originally published in the UK by Harold Pinter, with subsequent collections appearing in South Africa, Britain and America. Her poetry appears in local and overseas journals and anthologies. Gail has also written plays (Winner, SA PEN Millennium competition) and short stories (short-listed for the Thomas Pringle Award, 2010, long-listed for the Twenty in 20 Project 2014), and has recently completed her first novel. Gail pioneered Contemporary Dance in South Africa and was nominated for the inaugural AA Vita Award for Best Performer.

Abigail George was born into a family of educationalists in Port Elizabeth, raised and schooled in Swaziland and Johannesburg. She is not purely devoted to poetry but to pursuing writing full-time. Storytelling for her has always been a phenomenal way of communicating and making a connection with other people.

Sunelle Geyer (Swanepoel) was born in Kimberley in 1974, grew up in Boksburg and matriculated from the Afrikaanse Hoër Meisieskool Pretoria. She studied at the University of Pretoria and teaches intellectual property law at the University of South Africa. Her favourite timeout activities include reading fantasy novels, collecting perfume bottles, swimming, and spending time with her husband and their two daughters.

Kerry Hammerton lives in Cape Town. She has published poetry in South African and UK literary journals. Some of her poems were included in the anthologies *Difficult to Explain* (2010 Finuala Dowling), *Africa, My Africa* (2013

Patricia Schonstein) and *For a Rhino in a Shrinking World* (2013 Harry Owen). *These are the lies I told you*, her debut poetry collection, was published by Modjaji Books in 2010. *The Weather Report*, her second collection, was published in 2014. Kerry still has fewer wrinkles than she should have at her age – or so her friends tell her.

Vernon R.L. Head was born in 1967 in Cape Town in a bungalow near the sea (and near the gulls). He studied architecture, winning national and international awards for design and creative thinking. He is also chairman of BirdLife South Africa, one of Africa's biggest conservation organisations. When he is not designing strange buildings, he travels the world looking for the rarest birds. He is – essentially – a birdwatcher! His first book, a non-fiction narrative, *The Search for the Rarest Bird in the World* was published in by Jacana Media September 2014.

Colleen Higgs writes short fiction and poetry; she is also a publisher. She has had two collections of poems published: *Halfborn Woman* (2004) and *Lava Lamp Poems* (2011). *Looking for Trouble*, her first collection of short stories, was published in 2012. She started Modjaji Books for fun in 2007; since then it has become an internationally recognised and much-loved independent, feminist publishing company. She lives in Cape Town with her partner, her daughter, three dogs and a cat.

Sandra Hill is a writer and writing facilitator, working with civil society organisations as well as with those who write for the love of it (Write-Now). Her poetry and short stories have been published by New Contrast, Aerodrome, Jacana Media and Umuzi. Sandra, who lives in Jonkershoek,

Stellenbosch, has a Master's Degree (cum laude) in Creative Writing from The University of the Western Cape.

Rochelle Jacobs is a 23-year-old student in her final year at Stellenbosch University studying a BA in Politics, Philosophy and Economics. She is fairly old for a student but that's because she took four gap years where she spent some time overseas learning to fly helicopters but mostly working at a bookstore. Generally, she blames this indecisiveness on the fact that she's always been a writer – she just didn't know it yet. Her passions boil down to three things: helping the world, getting the adrenaline flowing and literature. Greatest among these is literature, but she finds that writing works best when all three are present.

Thabo Jijana is a writer whose work, as shown in the poems he submitted for this year's award, is informed by his upbringing in rural Eastern Cape. His poetry has appeared in several publications that include *New Contrast*, *The Kalahari Review*, *Poetry Potion*, and most recently (in book form) in the *2013 Sol Plaatje European Union Poetry Anthology*. He attempts, in his writings, to shine a light on extraordinary events, such that he highlights a truth about general life. A journalist by trade, Thabo lives in Port Elizabeth, the coastal city.

Justine Joseph is a scientist by training and a word person by profession. She has a BSc (Medical) Honours in Cell Biology and 12 years' experience as a journalist. She's the editor of the innovation newspaper, *Inside|Out* and co-author of the book *The Story of the Fly and How it Could Save the World* with enviro-entrepreneur Jason Drew – the pair are now completing a second book. In a parallel universe Justine is working on a collection of poems (two of which are being published in a love anthology) as well as a collaborative exhibition of poetry and photographic art for November 2014.

Moses Nzama Khaizen is the former Chief Editor of the Wits Student Newspaper at the University of the Witwatersrand. His poetry has appeared in journals like *Timbila* and *Poetry Potion*; in newspapers and magazines like *Sowetan*, *Shopsteward*, and *Loocha*; and anthologies *Voyages* (2003) and *New Pegasus* (2004). He has performed at various platforms including the National Arts Festival, and the Jozi Book Fair. In 2010, Moses self-published two anthologies of poetry, *U ya va rungula* (Xitsonga) and *When the Moon Goes to Rest* (English). He hails from Nkuri-Tomu village in Giyani.

Trudi Makhaya is an economist, writer and business strategist. She has published academic articles on competition economics and policy. She contributes commentary to various media platforms, writes a column for *Business Day* and blogs at www.mzansipreneur.com. Trudi holds an MBA and an MSc in Development Economics from Oxford University, where she studied as a Rhodes Scholar. She also holds degrees from the University of the Witwatersrand, including an MCom in Economics and a BCom (Law). Trudi has held roles at the Competition Commission, Deloitte, Genesis Analytics and AngloGold Ashanti.

Katise Mawela was born in Vaalhoek in Mpumalanga Province. Along with other Pulana people, he was forcefully removed from his ancestral home by the apartheid regime and dumped at Shatale in Bushbuckridge. He was only four years old. Katise has been writing poetry for as long as he can remember. Katise used to write and recite his poems during festivals like World AIDS Day when he was still a student nurse in Mapulaneng Hospital. His poems 'Geriatric Lament', 'Grazing Bull' and 'Ode to Shatale', to name just a few, graced the pages of *Tribute* magazine in the 1990s. His poem 'Written to a Mother' won the Tribute Sanlam Poetry Award in 1999.

Frank Meintjies is based in Johannesburg and currently works as an independent researcher and development consultant. Before that, for over two decades, he worked on development issues in various non-governmental organisations. Frank has also been active in the arts world through various initiatives and events, and through the writing of commentary. His poetry has featured in various anthologies. His articles on culture have dealt variously with film in the townships, the role of resource centres in communities, language issues and the role of arts in society.

Komiso Mfingo is a young African living in Cape Town. He was born in the Free State city of Welkom. He is well-travelled. He writes poetry that resonates with what he sees, feels or experiences. Komiso was born of a Xhosa family and still follows tradition to the proverbial 'T'.

Andrew Miller is a freelance writer and poet living and working in Johannesburg. He has performed poetry and given lectures on a variety of stages, from the Joburg hip hop underground to the *Daily Maverick* Gatherings, WITS Business School Lectures and the National Arts Festival. He and his wife ran a developmental art gallery and creative space in the city of Joburg for ten years, where they were part of a collective, offering free resources – from Internet access to office space and marketing services – to young artists across all genres.

Janine Milne achieved a degree in Theory of Literature with distinctions from the University of South Africa. Her passion for poetry has ensured a low-key job serving drinks in a waterfront restaurant. She likes to think of herself as a hyperpollysyllabicsesquipedalianist with a fascination with the magical power of the written word. She lives in Slaapstad with six cats (three feral), two dogs and her fiancé (semi-feral). Although she is rather protective of her 'little darlings', she aims to have her poetry collection venture out into the world.

Jackie Mondi is a South African woman, who is a writer, poet and teacher. She is fascinated by the power of the written word and strives to harness this power to change people's lives. Her writing has been published in *The Sol Plaatje European Union Poetry Anthology* (2011 and 2012), *Face of the Spirit: Illuminating a century of essays by South African Women*, *So Much to Tell Vol. 2: An anthology of South African women writing*, *Agenda*, *The South African Labour Bulletin*, *Wrapped* magazine; and quoted in the 2009 Budget Speech. Jackie lives in Johannesburg with her husband Lumkile and son Vuyo.

Nedine Moonsamy has completed her doctoral research at the University of the Witwatersrand and will continue her research journey as a postdoc fellow at Rhodes University. Her current academic interests include time, nostalgia and post-transitional South African literature.

Nick Mulgrew was born in Durban in 1990. He is an associate editor of *Prufrock* magazine, and has won national awards for his fiction and journalism. His poetry has been published throughout South Africa and the United States. He lives in Cape Town.

Christelle Mussmann is a 21-year-old female expressionist. She has always been fascinated with the beautiful yet frail power of words. Literature is enticing, but expression has always had a stronger grip on her. From a young age she learned to express emotions through words. She has never planned a piece of writing; she has simply let it flow from her soul into tangible form. She follows no structure, no rules. Those are governed only by her heart. From there on out, it becomes personal, it loses its sense of mere words, and it becomes a conscious emotion.

Eduan Naudé is originally from Mossel Bay, but these days plies his trade in Pretoria. Running the race as a rat by day and escaping reality as a poet by night, Eduan is still finding his feet within the literary world. As a student in 2010 some of his poems were published in *Penseel*, an annual Stellenbosch University student collection of poetry. More recently some of his poems have found their way into the *Sol Plaatje European Union Poetry Anthology Vol. III* published in 2013.

Pamela Newham has worked as an English teacher, magazine journalist and feature's editor. She has published three young-adult novels. *Three Blind Dates* was runner up in Maskew Miller Longman Literature Awards for 2010. *The Klipspringers* (Oxford University Press, South Africa) is on the Department of Basic Education's 2014 catalogue for grade

7. Her poems have been published in *Carapace*, *The Ground's Ear* and *Difficult to Explain*. Her poem, 'Third Beach, Port St Johns' was shortlisted for the Sol Plaatje European Union Poetry award for 2012. She lives in Hout Bay.

Sizakele Nkosi is a poet, guitarist and a mother. She is the founding member of House of Siza. She is a resident poet for the MoFaya Poetry Movement and *Divulge* (a creative space for artists to share and network on their projects). In 2007 she was one of the finalists in the international poet of the year competition in Michigan. In 2010 she welcomed the world to South Africa with poetry on Radio2000. She was part of the Spoken Word Project. She also took part in the 2012 Polokwane Literary Festival and in 2014, the Northern Cape Literary and Literature Festival.

Lazola Pambo is a poet, novelist and essayist. His published work has appeared in the *2012 Short Story Day Africa anthology*, *Poetry Potion Journal*, *2012 Pendle War Poetry collection* (United Kingdom), *Fundza Literacy Trust*, *New Asian Writing* (Thailand), *Moonlight Songs for Pa Nelson Mandela anthology* (published by the Society of Young Nigerian Writers), *Words and Images In Flight* (New York), *Bat Shat Poetry Journal*, and *Aji Magazine* (Mississippi), amongst others. Lazola's hobbies are reading both ancient and modern literature.

Thabo Seseane lives in Johannesburg and works mainly in Soweto as a surgeon. He is also a freelance writer with several blogs as well as an ebook entitled *Easy Weight Loss in 30 days*. He is about to publish a biography of his inspirational American high school teacher, who was formerly a 'bad boy'.

Francine Simon was born in 1990. She was the firstborn to Roman Catholic parents and grew up in Durban. She began writing poetic prose at fifteen. She completed her Master of Arts (summa cum laude) in Creative Writing at the University of KwaZulu-Natal in 2013. Her unpublished collection is called *Shadow Sounds*. She spent a year in China teaching the English language. Currently, her poetic influences include Kobus Moolman, Charles Bukowski and Tony Hoagland. Her writing has been described as bizarre, lyrical and experimental. She hopes to write a creative nonfiction collection in the near future.

Annette Snyckers is a visual artist and poet living in Cape Town. She studied languages (English, French and German) at the University of Pretoria and later Fine Art at Unisa. She was a high school teacher and translator before dedicating herself to the visual arts. She has lived in Switzerland and has travelled extensively. Every few years she spends three months in Paris in an artist's residency programme. At home she loves the African landscape in all its variety and moods. As a lover of language and literature, Annette has always written either for academic purposes or for pleasure. Some of her poems were published in *Difficult to Explain* edited by Finuala Dowling (Hands on Books 2010), in two previous *Sol Plaatje European Union Poetry Anthology* volumes, in *Carapace* and online on the Stellenbosch Literary Project's website.

Dianne Stewart's poem, 'This Poem', is included in the Speech and Drama Association of South Africa's English Syllabus (Festival 2011-2013). She has a BA (Honours) in African Languages, an MA in English (South African Literature) and an MA in Creative Writing (UCT). She has published over 30 books, some internationally. Her work has been translated into Danish, Norwegian, Swedish, French, Spanish, isiXhosa, isiZulu, Afrikaans and S. Korean. Her writing awards include the MML The Young Africa Award (YA short story) and The Indwe Risk/University of KZN alumni Short Story competition.

Jan Tromp was born in Cape Town in 1964. He graduated in law in 1986 then sold everything and left South Africa as crew on a sailing ship in an open-ended adventure. Amazed by the natural world but disturbed by his own lack of belonging in it as well as the injustice in South Africa, he was searching for his identity and purpose. After two years of travelling and teaching English in Europe and Asia he felt a clear call to return home. He lives with his wife and sons near Tzaneen where he continues to practise law and write.

Chantelle Gray van Heerden is currently a full-time PhD student in her final year. Her research is in the field of translation studies and investigates the politics, ethics and aesthetics of translation from a Deleuzo-Guattarian perspective. She also works as an editor, translator and copywriter, and writes short stories and book reviews. Her short stories 'Margie says' and 'When Princess Diana comes' were published in the *Darker Times Anthology, vol.6*, and 'The most tender place' was published in the *Adults Only* anthology. She is an avid reader of good literature and philosophy, and supports veganism and the liberation of animals.

Sue Woodward is a freelance writer and editor of educational material. She is passionate about poetry as a creative discipline and has been writing and reading poetry for many years. Under her first name of Susan Mahoney, she has been published in literary publications such as *Sesame* (1989/1992), *New Contrast* (1997) and *Carapace* (2007/2009). Recently she decided to begin publishing in her married name of Sue Woodward and her poems have appeared in *New Contrast* and *Aerodrome*. She lives in Muizenberg and is fortunate to be able to walk her dogs along the Zandvlei estuary in the company of flamingos.

Sithembele Isaac Xhengwana was born in 1972 around King William's Town. He studied at the University of Cape Town, qualifying with a Bachelor of Social Sciences (Honours) degree in sociology and a Master of Arts (Creative Writing). His first book, a novelette, was published by Buchu Books in 1991. His first collection of poems, *Scatter The Shrilling Bones*, was published by Lovedale Press in 2003. From 2003 to 2005 he lectured English and Creative Writing at the University of Fort Hare, where he was then registered for a Doctor of Literature and Philosophy degree. He is presently employed by Statistics South Africa as a deputy director.

What is the European Union (EU)?

The EU is a unique economic and political partnership between 28 European countries* that has delivered half a century of peace, stability and prosperity; helped raise living standards; launched a single European currency; and is progressively building a single Europe-wide market in which people, goods, services and capital move among Member States as freely as within a country.

Created in the aftermath of the Second World War, the first steps taken towards a union were to foster economic cooperation. Since then, the union has developed into a huge single market with the euro as its common currency. What began as a purely economic union has evolved into an organisation spanning all areas, from development aid to environmental policy.

The EU actively promotes human rights and democracy and has the most ambitious emission reduction targets for fighting climate change in the world. Thanks to the abolition of border controls between EU countries, it is now possible for people to travel freely within most of the EU.

How does it work?
EU Member States have set up institutions to run the EU and adopt its legislation. The main ones are:

---

* Belgium, Bulgaria, Croatia, Czech Republic, Denmark, Germany, Estonia, Ireland, Greece, Spain, France, Italy, Cyprus, Latvia, Lithuania, Luxembourg, Hungary, Malta, the Netherlands, Austria, Poland, Portugal, Romania, Slovenia, Slovakia, Finland, Sweden, and the United Kingdom.

- The European Parliament (representing the people of Europe)
- The Council of the European Union (representing national governments)
- The European Commission (representing the common EU interest)

Size & Population

The EU is less than half the size of the United States covering some 4 million km². In terms of size, France is the EU's largest country and Malta its smallest. The EU has a population of close to 503 million people – the world's third largest after China and India.

The EU's economy

Operating as a single market, the EU is a major world trading power. EU economic policy seeks to sustain growth by investing in transport, energy and research while minimising the impact of further economic development on the environment. Measured in terms of the goods and services it produces, its economy is bigger than that of the US: the EU GDP in 2012 was €12 945 402 million.

EU symbols

- The European flag – The 12 stars in a circle symbolise the ideals of unity, solidarity and harmony among the peoples of Europe.
- The European anthem – The melody used to symbolise the EU comes from Ludwig Van Beethoven 9th Symphony composed in 1823.
- Europe Day – The ideas behind the EU were first put forward on 9 May 1950 by French foreign minister

Robert Schuman. This is why 9 May is celebrated as a key date for the EU.
- The EU motto – "United in diversity".

The European Union & South Africa – a Partnership of Equals

Since 1994 the growing relationship between South Africa and the EU has been underpinned by the Trade, Development and Cooperation Agreement (TDCA). Closer ties between the two parties were consolidated in 2007 with the establishment of the EU-SA Strategic Partnership.

This Partnership, the only one of its kind with an African country, is centred on enhanced political dialogue around issues of shared interest including climate change, the global economy, governance, bilateral trade, and peace and security matters. In line with this, its action plan encompasses sectoral cooperation on a range of issues such as climate change, environment, education, science and technology, space, trade and migration, etc.

Annual summits, as well as ministerial and senior officials' meetings steer the Partnership, along with the EU-South Africa Joint Cooperation Council. They provide the occasions to discuss current bilateral, regional and global issues.

Trade & Investment

The EU remains South Africa's largest trading partner and in 2013 accounted for 25.57% of the value of South Africa's merchandise trade (import and exports). In turn, the EU, in value terms, remained the biggest source for South Africa's imports accounting for 29.29% of South Africa's total imports in 2013. EU countries are also the source of some 80% of foreign direct investment (FDI) stock in South Africa.

Development cooperation

The EU remains an important development partner to South Africa, providing significant external assistance funds. The EU's total indicative grant budget for South Africa for the period 2014–20 amounts to some €250 million. It is complemented by a €416 million loan finance envelope from the European Investment Bank (EIB) as well as grant funding from the EU Member States.